T0271671

How to Be
Curious

How to Be
Curious

Meena Alexander
and
STYLIST

First published in 2024 by Headline Home
an imprint of Headline Publishing Group

1

Cataloguing in Publication Data is available from the British Library

Hardback ISBN 978 1 0354 0472 8
eISBN 978 1 0354 0474 2

Typeset in 11/18pt FuturaFuturis by Jouve (UK), Milton Keynes

Printed and bound in Great Britain by Clays Ltd, Elcograf S.p.A.

MIX
Paper | Supporting
responsible forestry
FSC® C104740

Headline's policy is to use papers that are natural, renewable and recyclable
products and made from wood grown in well-managed forests and other
controlled sources. The logging and manufacturing processes are expected
to conform to the environmental regulations of the country of origin.

HEADLINE PUBLISHING GROUP
An Hachette UK Company
Carmelite House
50 Victoria Embankment
London EC4Y 0DZ

www.headline.co.uk
www.hachette.co.uk

Contents

CONTENTS

Foreword

By Lisa Smosarski, Editorial Director of Stylist

I was one of those children who was often called nosy. 'It's none of your business,' was a well-worn catchphrase in my home as my parents and brother swatted me away from investigating what was going on when they were chatting/reading/writing/on the phone/doing pretty much anything I wasn't involved in.

I don't think they were particularly secretive people, so I can only assume that my childish questioning was driving them up the wall – which you can probably relate to if you've ever been on the receiving end of a small child's external monologue. 'Why is your mouth so big?', 'What does God look like?' and 'Why are some people so mean?' are all questions I've been faced with from a small child recently, and my answers have been impatient and, I suspect, inadequate.

Looking back, like most children, those questions were an attempt to make sense of a world led by often abstract and illogical rules. I was determined to work it all out and can recall those random moments when I actually did, which were accompanied by a warm sense of gratification. Far from deterring me, my family's stock response may well have been the motivation I needed to quite literally *make* it my business to get people to answer my questions.

Journalism is the perfect career for anyone who is naturally curious.

As journalists, we are given permission to ask our questions all day long, and then spend the rest of our time searching for, and processing, the answers. I was fourteen when this eureka moment first hit me, thanks in part to a TV show called *Press Gang*, which was about a group of school kids making a newspaper. Each episode would see them hold truth to power – often their teachers or local people of note. They would bravely interrogate these people before discovering the truth and then causing real trouble by printing it. I decided that was my calling, and off I went to journalism school.

The reality of the job turned out to be even better than fourteen-year-old me had imagined. I was being paid to ask celebrities, MPs, businesspeople and fascinating humans questions about their lives and their work. I got to visit 10 Downing Street and Buckingham Palace, and to visit places that I thought I would only ever see on TV, drinking in every detail so I could share it with others. As I became an editor, it became my job to hypothesise on topics that baffled me – like 'Why do we still get colds?' and 'Is the weather really worse at weekends?' – and commission other journalists to come back to me with the answers (the results of both of these bits of analysis were published in *Stylist* and still remain some of my favourite reads). A good day at the office involved examining how my readers were feeling so I could produce the content they didn't even know they wanted. Every day was different, and I would revel in the pleasure of learning something new every week – like did you know that people sneeze differently depending on the language they speak? Just one of the many random facts I've retained from my commissions at *Stylist*.

My entire team at *Stylist* share this trait of insatiable curiosity. Some may call it nosiness or think what's private should remain that way, but I have only ever seen curiosity as an incredible power to think – or act – beyond that which we already know. It is an openness to the fact that we don't have all the answers or know how to do everything . . . and an ability to revel in the pleasure of trying to find out.

I have come to learn there are many different types of curiosity, ranging from emotional (questioning our own behaviours and why we feel what we feel), to practical (how do I fix, make or improve something or expand my skill set?), intellectual (philosophising and existential thought or desire for deeper knowledge), creative (exploring new practices, artistry and creation), scientific (proof and disproof or exploration of that which we want to know more about) and truth-finding (a suspicion there might be more to something than meets the eye and a desire to know more).

Scientists believe this natural-born curiosity is as essential to our survival as sleep, food and water, and have discovered that our body rewards us with a hit of dopamine, the feel-good hormone, when we sate our curiosity. Dopamine is normally associated with truly pleasurable moments – being given a gift or hugging a loved one, eating something tasty or even having great sex – yet curiosity triggers that same, pleasurable feeling, albeit perhaps in slightly lower levels.

Without curiosity, we would not have survived in evolutionary terms, which is why our DNA evolved to reward it. It is the ingrained curiosity that drives our ability to find food, water or shelter . . . or, more randomly, the innate need we feel to immediately touch a hot plate just after someone warns us not to. It is also presumably what led us to discover that we should run away from, not towards, a sweet-looking tiger or lion, and that some things taste much better – or make us less ill – when blasted with fire. Curiosity drives babies to discover they have feet and eventually to learn to walk, and helps adults to create coping mechanisms when faced with a crisis or conundrum.

Since our lives became less focused on running away from sabre-toothed tigers or finding a cave to sleep in, that dopamine hit is now much more likely to come from solving a tricky problem or discovering something new. Which means learning can, quite literally, make us feel genuine pleasure and happiness.

It is perhaps disappointing to discover then that, despite this great gift for deriving hormonal highs from knowledge, we are likely to become less curious as we age. One theory for why this happens as we mature is down to the sheer overwhelm adulthood can bring. When faced with stress, relationship troubles, career challenges, the toxicity of our polarised society, where curiosity can bring cancellation, or just the overwhelming news cycle itself, many people instinctively want to retreat away from the perceived 'danger'. But getting curious about how to tackle those challenges can be an antidote in itself. Seeking answers can empower us to find, if not solutions, then alternative workarounds or a more thorough understanding, which can then help us process what is going on.

As we age further, curiosity may also be replaced by a sense of wisdom, of having seen or done it all before. Yet a research paper in 2018 found that avoiding the temptation to give in to this and maintaining our natural-born curiosity can help stave off cognitive and physical decline as we age, with memory being specifically boosted by this curious mindset.

And that's not all. Countless studies have connected curiosity to increased engagement and enjoyment of work, a reduction in stress, burnout, anxiety and depression, strengthened relationships, and a generally more positive and happier mindset. Thankfully, we know you're a curious bunch. And it is this openness to being curious and new experiences that has sparked the growth of continuous learning, a new trend which sees us open our minds to ongoing and voluntary, self-motivated education. This form of learning isn't always traditionally academic and can be truly broad-ranging – from searching to understand someone else's experience in order to empathise or rethink your own position, to learning a new skill, like shoe-making or upholstery – and has the power to awaken our natural curiosity, which is often eroded by our busy lives and never-ending to-do lists.

I am a firm believer in the saying 'If you're comfortable, you're not learning,' and the same goes for curiosity too. If you think you have all the answers, you've probably stopped asking the right questions. So let *How to Be Curious* become your new playbook for wriggling into that discomfort zone and reigniting that once-annoying but now quite inspired inner-child who asked 'why?' and 'how?' on repeat until they got the answers they were looking for. The topics in this book, created by our Features Director Meena Alexander and her army of experts, are here to inspire and motivate you to renew your curiosity and squeeze more of the juice out of life. Take this chance to look at the world through a different lens and, if you do nothing else, just stay curious.

A note on journaling

Throughout this book you will be asked to journal, a method proven to consolidate learning and help process your thoughts as you come across new ideas and self-discovery tools. Look out for prompts and questions within each chapter – and keep your favourite notebook and a pen handy.

RELATIONSHIPS

1. Should friendships be hard work?

For decades, friendships have seemed to play second fiddle to romantic relationships. Where practically every film, book or TV show centred on a meet-cute or lovers' quarrel, only a few put platonic relationships at the heart of their narratives. They weren't deemed important or life-altering enough, a secondary tier of relationship that many people took for granted.

But anyone who's ever had a friend make them laugh when they needed it most, met someone who instantly 'gets' them, or felt the heartbreak of a friendship on the rocks knows how wrong that is. There is little more vital to a well-lived life than true friendship. Many people can, and plenty of people do, spend their lives without a long-term romantic partner, but few could survive without friends.

Science shows that having a handful of good friends has extraordinary effects on your quality of life and wellbeing, accounting for sixty per cent of the difference in an individual's happiness, regardless of whether they're an introvert or an extrovert. In a study of 'superagers' (men and women over eighty whose memories are as good as or better than those of people twenty to thirty years younger) by Northwestern University, the superagers stood out in one area only: the degree to which they reported having satisfying, warm, trusting relationships. Good friends lift you up, cheer you on and drag you over the finish line if you need them to.

The friendship masterclass:
Five ways to stay close
by Marisa Franco

There are things you can do – both big and small – to encourage
a meaningful, long-lasting bond with the people you care about.
Marisa Franco, friendship expert and psychologist, sheds light
on how to preserve and deepen our friendships with five tried-
and-tested methods.

1. Be vulnerable, even if it's against your instincts

It's sometimes one of the hardest things in the world, but in order
to ensure that your friendship has the legs to survive what life will
throw at it, it's important to be vulnerable with your friends.
According to Franco, it 'generates intimacy'. 'People actually like
us more when we're vulnerable because it conveys that we trust
and like them,' she says. While it can be easy to assume that
vulnerability comes hand in hand with perceived weakness,
Maria argues that with friends, this is often not the case – in fact,
the opposite is true. 'Friends see us more positively than we
assume – they see us as authentic and honest when we are
vulnerable,' she says.

One thing you could practise is 'scaffolding vulnerability' –
start out talking and acting in a vulnerable manner with someone
you are closest to, and then, once you've had a good response,
extend those exercises to your relationships with others who are
newer to your inner circle. 'This is going to feel a lot less scary
and a lot less risky to you, because you already feel more secure

from that initial scaffolding,' Franco says. 'So if you feel comfortable talking to a sibling or a parent, but you haven't necessarily built that up with your friends, start there, and then share with your friends – and then [you can] open up to someone who's a bit more of a wild card.'

2. Make sure you 'repot' your friendships

Franco offers a really beautiful way of looking at your relationships with your friends – tend to them like you would a potted plant. Franco advises that we 'vary the settings' in which our friendships take place. 'So if you start going to the movies with them, or you take a trip with them, all of that is going to deepen friendships simply by shaking up things you do together,' she explains. This helps with the prevention of the classic downfall of any relationship, getting 'stuck in a rut', based on a principle called self-expansion theory.

'We are all looking for ways to expand ourselves,' Franco says. 'And the number-one way we do that is through our relationships, through new experiences in our relationships.' This is a really fun, fulfilling way for both you and your friend to future-proof your relationship. This is a particularly good way to ensure that workplace relationships pass the test of time; when you inevitably move forward in your careers and perhaps away from each other.

'Asking a work friend for a walk, or for a fun non-work-related activity, can really change the dynamic of the relationship, because you're saying, "Hey, I'm invested in you, not just because we share a common workplace, but because I'm invested in you as a person",' she says.

3. Show a little affection, even if it seems weird

This one may seem obvious, or verging on awkward at times, but demonstrating to your mate just how much they mean to you has a lot of power. There's even a theory for it, Franco explains – risk regulation theory. 'The idea of risk regulation theory is that we will only invest in relationships if the risks of rejection are regulated,' she says. 'So basically, we only invest in our relationships when someone makes us feel safe to do that. And so when we affirm our friends, when we tell them, "I like you, you're so great, I'm so happy for you, I'm in your corner", what that does is it makes them feel safe to invest in us.

'So it kind of creates this upward, positively reinforcing cycle, where we can more easily keep our friendships alive.' Of course, everyone shows affection in different ways – and not always with words. Franco encourages you to have a think about which of the five love languages – acts of service, gift-giving, physical touch, words and quality time – would work best to convey your connection to your friends.

4. Never forget the importance of 'showing up'

When our friends need support, whether that involves something big or small, it's really important to ensure you are there for them when they need you – either physically, in person, or on the other end of a phone. Your friends will remember this, and it will 'solidify and cement' your friendship in a way that will strengthen it over time, according to Franco.

'Support is really a portal to deep intimacy,' she says, adding that it's important to step through that portal when we are invited. Franco stresses that when we support our friends, we are helping to strengthen a friendship and increasing its durability over time because it makes us 'more optimistic' during periods of being out of touch or more distant because you already have such a strong history.

When this closeness is fostered with a friend, their presence and personality become part of us and our sense of self, which Franco classes as part of a term called the 'inclusion of the self'. 'So it feels like they're with us all the time,' she says. 'It allows you to live through periods of separation from friends, because it doesn't feel as much like you are – you've incorporated them into your sense of self, becoming central to who you are.'

5. Remember that longevity isn't always possible

If you become close friends with someone very quickly and it doesn't end up lasting very long, it may be that the entire relationship lacked the required foundation from the beginning, Franco says. 'Sometimes friendships that are super intimate have a shorter life because they've built up too quickly,' she says. 'All of that intimacy makes you increase your expectations in a way that can ultimately make the friendship fail. So I think moving slowly in friendship is a good idea,' she recommends.

That said, it's really important to stress that every friendship is important in its own way, big or small. Franco stresses that while these close relationships can 'reflect our identities', our identities can evolve so that we don't connect with our loved ones anymore. 'It's normal for this to happen,' she says. In fact, research finds that the average person replaces half their friends every seven years. We can honour the friendship for what it gave us at a certain time in our lives without it having to last forever. 'We can also use the friendship ending as an invitation for us to explore how our identity – or our friend's – has changed and what our needs are in relationships going forward.'

The secret to making friends as an adult

So, what about starting from scratch? Making friends in adulthood can be daunting; it's no longer as simple as sidling up to someone in the playground and offering them one of your jelly babies. A global 2019 study by Snapchat called The Friendship Report discovered that the average age at which we meet our best friends is twenty-one: an age when we're starting to become the people we want to be, but are still open to all the wonders and possibilities that lie ahead. We do tend to think about close friendships in terms of longevity, calling the people who know us because of time and circumstance – say, we grew up on the same street or were on the same course at university – our very best friends. But fulfilling connections can be made at any stage in life – they may just take a little more open-mindedness and effort to spark.

Why is it worth making new friends throughout my life?
Naturally, as we get older, we can lose the friends we once had due to shifting priorities or lifestyle differences. But it is important to replenish our stocks, to find friends on our wavelength with whom we share values and experiences, and who really understand us. Having the company and support of someone who cares about you is scientifically proven to make life easier. In one American study, when

a group of female students were asked to complete challenging maths tasks, their heart rates went up – a sign of stress. But when they were asked to complete the tasks with a friend in the room, their heart rates were lower. Similarly, scientists know that when monkeys are moved to a new environment, the level of stress hormones in their blood spikes, but when their preferred companion is with them, the level of stress hormones is much lower. Emotional burdens are far less difficult to bear when the load is shared with a friendly and familiar face.

Arguably, it becomes more important to have a social circle around us as we head for old age. Even more so than a romantic partner, good friends are key to good health: a ten-year Australian study found that older people with a large circle of friends were a whopping twenty-two per cent less likely to die than those who just had a few. In areas of the world where people live far longer than the average life expectancy (often referred to as 'Blue Zones'), friendships seem to play an important role. For example, in Okinawa, Japan, where female life expectancy is the highest in the world at ninety (in the UK, we're currently sitting at around eighty-two), people form a social network called a 'moai' – a group of five friends who share resources such as crops and money when needed, but also offer each other emotional support for a lifetime. Forging connections with people you can count on may well be the best thing you can do for your mental and physical health.

So how do I meet new people?

It can be trickier to make friends in adulthood when so many people already have their set social circles, more responsibilities and a busy schedule, but it's far from impossible – and more people are open to it than you think. Here are a handful of ways to expand your circle.

Do your kind of thing to meet your kind of people

Think about the things that make your heart sing: the subject you could wax lyrical about for hours; the activity you can see yourself doing for decades to come. Pursuing a passion, whether it's joining a club or team, going to specialised events or joining group trips, will not only bring out an excited and vibrant side of you that's attractive to other people, but it'll also throw you into situations where you'll meet people who are into the same things you are. Take advantage of this ready-made commonality and see what else you might like about each other.

Swipe right

Friendship apps are becoming more popular among young women, who are increasingly seeking like-minded people to spend time with and shedding the false narrative that to actively seek out friends is something to be ashamed about. Download an app like Bumble BFF, Peanut or Gofrendly, where you can organise platonic dates based on other people's profiles, interests and hobbies. If you ever feel odd or embarrassed, just remember that everyone else you come across will be in exactly the same boat. It's a judgement-free zone.

Be open to the unexpected

Try to be open-minded to the idea that your next great friendship is just round the corner, and don't see the pursuit of new friends as a slight to your old ones. If you're at an event, avoid huddling away with the people you already know; use the safety net of knowing them to bolster your confidence in talking to new people. Pay attention to the kernels of connection you may already have, too: don't write off an acquaintance or a neighbour you've bumped into a few times just because it hasn't organically blossomed into something more. Invite them out for a coffee and see if you get along well – you might already know your new best friend, you just haven't watered that seed yet.

Be proactive

Often, we're so worried about rejection or 'coming on too strong' that we end up doing nothing at all, but friendships worth having aren't forged out of thin air. If you find someone funny or notice something about them that you admire, speak up and tell them. If you want to get to know someone better or are interested in their opinions, ask them. As a general rule, people are flattered when someone shows interest in them, so you'll be off to a good start.

I've met someone I can see myself being friends with – what now?

Meet somewhere neutral

In the early stages of getting to know someone, it's worth suggesting a meet-up spot where you both feel relaxed and can focus on each other, rather than at one of your homes, where you or your new friend might feel under pressure to be a good host. If you already know you have a shared interest, suggest a friend date that incorporates it: say, a concert by a musician you both like or a game of tennis. This gives you something to springboard off when it comes to conversation.

Ask questions

And really listen to the answers. In the early stages of any relationship, we're constantly trying to read the signals that point to the other person's intentions, to figure out if they're actually interested in us or have some other agenda. Showing that you care about your new friend's experiences and opinions is key to creating a bond.

Don't expect too much

Heaping pressure on one person to be the answer to all your friendship woes is likely to make the budding relationship crumble, as can trying to accelerate things too fast. Trust and familiarity can take a while to build, so be patient and enjoy the process of getting to know someone new – you'll naturally arrive at a level of closeness that suits both of you.

Why we should all be better at arguing

We've all had them: the friendships that turn sour, going from fun and supportive to the name you dread popping up on your phone screen. Sometimes, life can pull two people in different directions or we evolve in different ways from our friends, bringing the relationships to a natural end. But other times it's less clear cut; something has gone wrong, be it a one-off argument or an ongoing awkwardness, and it's hard to know how to get past it.

'When conflict in friendships occurs, it can be really hard to handle,' says Grace McMahon, a life coach at Being Well Family. 'If an issue within a friendship is causing you anxiety, it's something that you need to address,' she continues, explaining that this is true even if it is something that you consider trivial. 'Friends bicker and communicate in unusual ways, which can be OK as long as it works for you and isn't causing you stress,' McMahon explains. 'But if the way you and a friend communicate makes you feel like you don't want to spend time with them or it's causing a problem for you personally, you need to address it.' If you find yourself in an uncomfortable spot with a friend, try these steps to salvage the situation – it's almost always worth it.

Clarity is key

Ask yourself, what exactly is it that's putting a strain on your relationship? Identify the issue, whether it's an annoying habit of theirs, something they've done or said that hurt you, or a lack of effort or care. Whatever it is, be very clear in your own mind about the problem and consider whether or not you feel it's something your friend can actually help you address, rather than your own insecurity or bugbear, before you bring it to them.

McMahon recommends that you make physical notes before confronting a friend. 'Make a few bullet points in a notebook or on your phone about what you want to say and why you need to say it,' she advises. 'This will help to make you feel less stressed, which can help you put your point across in a more amicable way. This will also stop your friend from feeling defensive.' McMahon says that it's totally fine to have your notes with you while talking to your friend. You can explain that having them with you makes you feel less anxious about the situation, and a good friend will understand this.

Choose a safe space

'Texting someone is an immediate invitation for misinterpretation and fuel for conflict,' McMahon says, explaining that meeting someone in person to discuss an issue is the best route, with a phone call being the other option to consider if you can't meet someone in person. 'Make sure you find somewhere to meet where you both feel comfortable,' she goes on, suggesting one of your homes or a coffee shop that you're both familiar with.

It can be useful to have these discussions in public because that means you're both on equal footing in terms of how comfortable you are in the space. However, if you do think you need to express a lot of emotion in order to resolve the issue, it might be best to have the discussion in one of your homes, McMahon advises. 'In public, you'll try not to cause a scene, but sometimes an outburst of emotions is just what you need in order to be heard and understood,' she says.

Tell them how you feel

Just as open, honest communication is crucial in a romantic partnership, it's crucial in a friendship to avoid resentments building up or the two of you being on different pages. Don't be afraid of voicing an issue to your friend – if it's done in a considerate and calm way, they should be receptive. Using 'I' statements to express how the issue is affecting you will keep it from turning nasty.

'When we talk about a problem, we often think we've explained it really well because we know exactly what's happening,' McMahon says. 'But you need to always check in with yourself that you're making things as clear as possible.' Over-explaining can be helpful when it comes to avoiding the defence mechanism of putting up walls. 'Often we'll shrug things off when we're faced with conflict, which is unhelpful in the long term,' McMahon explains. 'If you catch yourself doing that, just stop and explain to the other person that you didn't mean to shrug that off and that, actually, it is something that makes you uncomfortable.' It might seem silly to go back on yourself, but if you don't, this issue will keep on happening, so it's better to deal with it there and then, and sometimes this requires making yourself vulnerable.

Try to switch your perspective

When someone, or something in particular, has upset you, it can be easy to only see things from your own point of view. But this is unhelpful during disagreements. 'It's hard to be the bigger person, but it can be so helpful to step into the other person's shoes,' McMahon says, explaining that this will help you make fairer points and come to a resolution quicker.

'Do more listening than talking' is another thing she advises in order to help you empathise with your friend. It's key to focus on the situation at hand and avoid bringing up things from the past, which can cause unnecessary drama and escalate the situation. If you need to take some time to calm down before you speak to your friend, then do so. 'If you're in a calm and collected mindset, that will be far more helpful than starting a conversation in the heat of the moment,' she explains.

The best way to speak about conflict, according to McMahon, is to state the problem and explain how it's making you feel and then listen to the other person's response. 'A lot of the time, we try and guess how other people feel, so making the time to really listen to them is key,' she explains.

Give the friendship space to evolve

Nothing will change overnight, so give your friend time to process and take on board what you've said. Be sure to play your part in overcoming the issue, too. For example, if you feel your friend hasn't been there for you enough, be vocal about what you need from them and allow them the space to show up for you the next time. It's also worth being open to the fact that friendships will shift and change over time; just because you see your friend less or are tending to talk more about work at the moment, it doesn't necessarily mean you're less close. It may just be a symptom of your respective lives.

Try not to get others involved

Particularly if you share mutual friends or are part of a group, it can be hard not to drag others into the issues between two people, but generally doing this can muddy the water. Everyone has their own perspective or opinion, but it's more helpful to focus on your own – how does this friendship make you feel, and what do you want it to look like moving forward? Although it can be helpful to lean on other friends or ask for advice, be careful of that getting back to the person in question. If they catch wind of gossip or feel like people are 'taking sides', it could damage your relationship and drive you further apart.

Set new boundaries if you need to

A lack of boundaries is often the root cause of many issues that arise within friendships. So, if you've been able to resolve the issue at hand, a good next step is to put some new boundaries in place with your friend to prevent further conflict in the future. 'We need boundaries to protect ourselves, and putting them in place with a friend shouldn't upset them if you explain why you need them,' McMahon says.

   The boundaries you put in place will be very personal, but they're often based around communication. For example, you might need to set some rules about the ways in which you communicate and how often you communicate. 'You have to be quite strong-willed with boundaries,' she explains, noting that you will have to check in with yourself to make sure you're keeping them in place.

McMahon also explains that it's important to make sure you don't offer your availability to someone when you're not actually available. In order to be polite, you might tell your friends that you're always there for them if they need you, or that they can call you at any time. But if you aren't at a point where you *can* be there for them all the time, this will only cause more issues. It's best to be honest with friends about what you can put into that relationship right now and, if that is very little, to tell them that you'll come back to them when you have more to offer. 'You have to prioritise looking after yourself, because you can't be there for other people if you're not OK yourself,' McMahon says.

Know when to throw in the towel

Ultimately, a friend should be a source of comfort, support and love in your life. If someone is making you feel bad or you dread spending time with them, that's a sure-fire sign that the friendship is no longer fit for purpose. It's never a good idea to write someone off over one or two misdemeanours, but you're also well within your rights to break off a friendship that's become toxic – know your own boundaries and know you deserve friends who care about you and show it. Often, a friendship that's run its course might fizzle out on its own, but if you want to be clear and ensure a clean break, let them know why you'll no longer be reaching out, keeping communication kind and civil. Then you know you've done your bit.

Friendship red flags to look out for

- **Being overly critical or insulting:** It might seem like an obvious one, but often it's the people closest to us who can treat us badly for a long time before we really notice it. Nit-picking or little insults that start off as a 'joke' might descend into full-blown character assassination, making you feel low and unappreciated. A person who makes you feel this way is not your friend. They're probably doing it out of their own insecurity, but that doesn't mean you need to put up with it.

- **Trauma dumping:** Friendship means supporting each other through difficult times, but occasionally a friend can veer into unhealthy territory by using you as a vessel to download all their darkest feelings without warning or invitation. It's important to have boundaries with your friends – you don't owe them emotional availability at the expense of your own mental wellbeing, and it's not your job to shoulder their burdens without any support of your own.

- **Competitiveness:** If you can't mention one of your achievements without your friend immediately belittling it or trying to one-up you, they may have an issue with jealousy. This can be a tricky dynamic to address, but if it starts to get you down, it's not worth sticking around. A true friend should be able to celebrate your wins or at least communicate why they're finding it hard to.

- **Flakiness:** Sometimes we have friends who we've consigned to the 'unreliable' drawer, who often opt out of plans last minute or rarely come through for us when we need them most. If it only happens for a short stint, it may just be down to something going on in their own lives, but in the long term, it doesn't make for a friendship based on mutual care and respect.

How deep listening can help us have constructive arguments
by Louisa Weinstein

There is a difference between 'listening to understand' and 'listening to respond', and we often end up doing the latter. Deep listening is a technique that encourages us to empathise with another person's point of view. Here's an expert guide on how to use the technique to have more constructive arguments and be more open-minded from Louisa Weinstein, a conflict mediation specialist and the founder of The Conflict Resolution Centre, and Caroline Plumer, a BACP-accredited therapist and founder of CPPC London.

Disagreement is a natural part of life, but it's not unusual to be in a situation where we find it hard to even speak to someone whom we adamantly believe is wrong. From social media spats to polarised political views, it can often feel like we're living in divided times. But, whether it's a debate about Brexit or a domestic squabble about whose turn it is to take out the bins, debates can get heated and become deadlocked when we come from two opposing sides, even if the person in question is someone we love and respect.

Much of the time, stalemates come about because we're not actually listening to another person's opinion. In fact, the simple act of listening to someone properly can be the difference between a fruitful discussion and an impasse. This is where a technique called deep listening comes in. Deep listening is a form of empathetic listening, where we establish trust with the person we're talking to by trying to understand their point of view.

'When we practise empathetic listening with the intention to really understand the other person and we are prepared to hear a different perspective, there is always an opportunity for a solution,' says Weinstein. What's more, deep listening is something we can get better at over time. 'Deep listening is a skill that can be honed and developed,' adds Plumer. 'If you practise it, you will get better at it and it will start to become more natural in all kinds of situations.'

What is deep listening?

Deep listening is distinct from normal listening because it requires people to enter a conversation with the intention of connecting with someone and establishing trust. The technique has a lot of crossover with active listening. An idea developed by American psychologist Carl Rogers, active listening involves paraphrasing or repeating back what someone has said as well as responding to their body language. These behaviours mean we can listen to someone more carefully and fully.

Deep listening takes active listening a step further by involving empathy. 'Deep listening is a mindful approach to listening,' says Plumer.

Weinstein adds, 'It focuses on empathy and making sure from the outset you're listening to someone in a non-judgemental way. You're putting yourself in their position and you're listening to learn. Generally, when we scrap with someone, we adopt a childlike state,' says Weinstein. 'Even political debates can be very childlike and end up being patronising and condescending. When we employ deep listening, we start behaving differently and move into an adult state, which is objective and able to see the full picture.'

Research published in the *National Journal of Medical Research* also finds that when we are listened to deeply, it makes us feel more valued and accepted, even if we don't agree with the person we're talking to.

How to practise deep listening

1. Enter discussions with an intention

Deep listening is most effective when a conversation has a clear objective, and this doesn't necessarily mean 'winning' a discussion in the traditional sense. 'When you enter a discussion, go in with an intention to understand the other person and be prepared to hear a different perspective,' says Weinstein.

'A good starting point for deep listening is asking yourself what you want from a discussion and what is a good outcome. It could be to preserve a relationship or to have dignity in a relationship because that's the first thing we start to lose when things unravel,' Weinstein adds.

In many discussions or debates, the intention is to 'win'. However, when we employ deep listening, winning doesn't always mean trouncing the other person. 'Coming out on top isn't necessarily winning the argument,' explains Weinstein. 'You need to go beyond that. Winning might mean being the bigger person or finding a better alternative. That's when deep listening is most powerful – when it creates change.'

2. Ask open questions

Asking open questions helps us understand another person's point of view more fully. 'The questions you ask are as important, maybe more important, than the listening,' says Weinstein. These questions will also give your conversation structure, which is important for deep listening. Weinstein recommends asking the other person these questions:

- 'What do you want?'
- 'What does that look like specifically?'
- 'Could you tell me more about what you want?'
- 'What are the milestones to achieving that?'
- 'What would need to happen for you to get what you want?'
- 'What will happen when you get what you want?'

'The first time someone says something is not usually their full answer,' explains Weinstein. 'So repeating the question can give you a better understanding of what someone is saying. These questions are useful because we often don't think through getting the outcome that we want. If we really think about it, we might not want it in the first place.'

3. Repeat back what people have said

Paraphrasing or repeating back what a person has said is a key component of active listening, but it can also be used to enhance deep listening. Repetition reinforces the speaker's message and shows we're trying to understand them. 'If you clarify by repeating back what someone is saying, you will make them feel at ease and make them feel heard,' says Plumer. 'It reduces the likelihood of crossed wires. It also means the person will become more receptive because they feel really heard by you. Repetition can feel silly, but it ends up being really powerful. Particularly when you've known someone a long time, you can assume you know what they're thinking or feeling. Paraphrasing gives a feeling that the other person is trying to really listen to you and understand your experiences.'

4. Avoid interrupting and giving advice

Previous studies have emphasised the difference between 'listening to understand' and 'listening to respond'. While many of us believe we listen effectively, it is in fact human nature to spend conversations planning what we are going to say next or thinking of solutions to people's problems instead of trying to understand them.

'A lot of the time, even if we're not interrupting someone, often we will be thinking about what we want to say next. We're almost just waiting our turn and looking for the next opportunity to speak,' says Plumer. Deep listening aims to put this to one side so we can be as open and receptive to someone as possible.

Plumer adds that giving out advice to someone you're speaking to is counterproductive to deep listening. 'Think about yourself in their position, rather than just doling out advice. A lot of the time when people give advice, it comes from a really good place, but they haven't taken the time to understand all of the circumstances and the feelings that might be happening to the other person.'

5. Develop trust and build a comfortable space

In the same way laughter is infectious, as soon as one person employs deep listening it can rub off on the people you are talking to. A huge part of deep listening is creating a trusting and comfortable space so people are able to speak freely. As soon as this is achieved, people feel calmer and less explosive, prompting more constructive discussions.

'The bottom line is feeling comfortable enough to open up,' says Weinstein. 'You're not going to go into something deeply or be open to new perspectives unless you feel comfortable [enough] to do that.'

'If you show the other person empathy and really engage with them, you'll find you get a much better response from people,' adds Plumer. 'If you go in with a good attitude, most people will be really receptive and try to meet you in the middle.'

6. Be brave and prepare to hear different opinions

Practising deep listening can be uncomfortable. It means we may be confronted with things we disagree with or we may be challenged on our beliefs. 'You have to be very brave when you use deep listening,' says Weinstein. 'Deep listening requires us to really reflect on our beliefs and opinions and, without sounding trite, means we really have to face our fears.

'It also requires us to take personal responsibility, which is very hard. Not only do we have to be prepared not to be right, but conflicts shine a light on our vulnerabilities and least pleasant traits. Unless we're prepared to take responsibility for them, it's harder to work through the process.'

Journal prompts to help you reflect on the friendships in your life

- *What do you appreciate about the friendships you made in childhood?*
- *What do you appreciate about the friendships you've made in adulthood?*
- *If you could change one thing about your social circle, what would it be?*
- *When was the last time you lost a friend, and what did you learn from it?*
- *When was the last time you were vulnerable with a friend, and how did it make you feel?*
- *If you're having a tough day, who is the first person you want to talk to and why?*
- *With whom do you feel most like yourself?*
- *What is something a friend has done for you recently that made you feel loved?*
- *What could you do for a friend this week to make them feel loved?*
- *How would you like your friends to describe you?*

2. How people-pleasing holds us back

Do you tend to agree with people, even when deep down you don't really mean it? Do you struggle to say no — to going to events, to taking on extra tasks at work — even when you know you should refuse? Have you been known to apologise often, even for things that are out of your control? Do you feel unsettled or guilty when people around you are unhappy, and compelled to try and fix it?

If your answer to any of these questions is yes, you may well have some people-pleasing tendencies. 'People-pleaser' is a signifier that's thrown around a lot, but it can be a difficult thing to identify in ourselves. Often, we confuse it with simply being kind or selfless, assuming that to constantly edit our own opinions and behaviours in favour of keeping others happy is a positive attribute, rather than a damaging one. But there is a difference between being a good person and being a people-pleaser: the former takes other people into consideration, yes, but doesn't ignore their own wants and needs in the process. *This* is where the problem with people-pleasing arises: we come last.

Supporting others is a key part of positive relationships, but when we put ourselves on the backburner for too long, it can have a major impact on our mental health and sense of self. But the fact is, we live in a world that encourages us to put others first — especially if we're women.

'Women have less margin to be displeasing, because we're taught that so much of our worth is wrapped up in pleasing others,' explains Natalie Lue, writer, podcaster and author of *The Joy of Saying No*. 'It starts so young, when we're separated into the "good" girls and boys and the "bad" girls and boys. And those labels are totally dependent on how compliant and obedient you are – basically, how pleasing you are to the adults around you.'

In this way, many of us learn people-pleasing as a sort of survival strategy: smile and nod politely, say the things your authority figures want to hear, keep any impulsivity or mischievousness to yourself and you will be labelled 'good'.

'What happens is, we get to adulthood and we continue to try and use these survival habits, but they become increasingly ineffective,' explains Lue. 'As time goes on, you find you're experiencing more and more repercussions for your people-pleasing – you're frustrated, burned out, overwhelmed – but it's confusing because there was a time when it probably worked well for you.'

We often think of people-pleasing in extremes. Some might think it means they're a total 'doormat' while others might feel it makes them very virtuous, but the vast majority of us are somewhere in between, with suspicions that we might be people-pleasing in certain situations but unsure why or how to get out of the habit. There's no shame in recognising that you're a people-pleaser, but you do need to recognise it, because the effects on your wellbeing and the quality of your relationships can be far-reaching.

Why is people-pleasing a problem?

In a nutshell, putting others before yourself results in a critical lack of self-care. If you're always doing things for others even when you've reached the point of overwhelm, you can begin to live under chronic stress and eventually burn out, whether that be in your professional or personal life. One symptom of this is that the inner voice that represents your most authentic self – the one that knows what you really want and need in any particular moment – gets turned down to almost nothing. It can become harder to connect with your own desires when you've become so used to ignoring them, and this means your sense of who you are can feel adrift.

'People-pleasing is a manifestation of a kind of anxiety, whether that's anxiety that you won't be liked or anxiety that you're not good enough,' says Lue. 'So we attempt to manage that anxiety by getting out in front of it and doing whatever we can to be liked or to prove we are good enough. The problem is, we're never quite sure it's working.' Constantly seeking approval and external validation, rather than having a healthy self-esteem fed by our own belief, can be an exhausting way to live. Like running on a hamster wheel and never getting anywhere, no matter how much you people-please, you can never get to the place of feeling 'good enough' if that conviction only comes from other people.

Perhaps the most ironic issue with people-pleasing behaviour is that despite the fact we're bending over backwards for the people around us, it can massively hinder the quality of our relationships. People-pleasers are notoriously bad at asking for help or voicing what they need from others, which you might assume makes you an easier person to be around, but actually results in one-sided relationships. Vulnerability and mutual support enrich connection, but it's difficult to do if you're terrified of being a 'burden' to your friends and loved ones.

Why do some of us become people-pleasers?

'It's a behaviour that generally begins in childhood, due to a family dynamic where being pleasing was a shortcut to love or approval,' explains Lue. It can also be a response to a major trauma or stress point in your life, a subconscious way to try and avoid conflict or further challenges by managing the emotions of everyone around you. As Lue explains, it is a behaviour rooted in fear, and for that reason we shouldn't be too hard on ourselves for falling into people-pleasing habits – particularly in times of stress. Discussing these habits and digging in to where they might have come from is best done with a trained professional, such as a counsellor or psychotherapist, who can create a safe and open environment.

What are the signs of a people-pleaser?

You say yes when you really mean no

A 'yes' can relate to anything that you agree to, be it lending someone money or going along with another person's opinion. But if it doesn't come from your heart or your own conviction, it's likely to be a people-pleasing response.

'Say somebody asks you to do something or says they need your help. Outwardly you say, "Yes, sure, no problem", but inwardly you're thinking, "Oh my goodness, don't they realise how much I've got on, how can I possibly manage this?"' explains Lue. 'Another scenario you might recognise: you're invited to an event and immediately you agree to go while simultaneously trying to figure out how you'll be able to get out of it at some point in the future.' Ironically, we tend to agree to avoid discomfort in the moment, but we're creating more work for ourselves down the line. 'Ask yourself: are you saying yes because you really want to and you're consciously consenting, or is it because you're trying to avoid something else: conflict, rejection, criticism?' says Lue. It can become a reflex to just say yes and deal with the consequences later, even when your internal voice is saying you don't have the capacity or desire to.

You're constantly seeking approval

Being overly concerned with how other people view you and whether they like you can be a sign of people-pleasing. Your sense of self-worth might hinge on what others say about you and how they respond to you, rather than a core belief that you are a decent and worthy person. This can set you on an emotional roller coaster of ups and downs, with how you're feeling depending on whether the people around you are praising you and seem happy with you, or whether they have expressed disappointment or upset relating to something you've said or done. You might experience a euphoric high when someone validates you, but feel utterly shaken by a criticism and unable to stop dwelling on it.

You regularly experience the 'people-pleaser emotions'

'The classic people-pleaser feelings are: resentment, guilt, anxiety, overwhelm, powerlessness [and] frustration,' says Lue. 'These feelings let you know that even if you're saying yes to a good thing, you're saying yes for the wrong reasons or you're doing it at the expense of your own wellbeing. If you regularly experience these feelings, it could be your body's way of telling you that you're agreeing to things in a way that lacks integrity or consideration of your own needs.'

Resentment is often one of the easiest to spot: an underlying, begrudging feeling that you're doing too much for others without the appropriate amount of gratitude or recognition in return, never mind the fact they don't know you're going against your deeper instincts. Overwhelm, too, is a key sign that you're physically and mentally putting yourself through more than you can handle, and ignoring your own need for rest and self-care. When these alarm bells go off, listen to them.

You have a very specific role in your relationships

'You might see your ability to keep everyone happy as the thing that makes you valuable or gives you purpose, and this feeds into the role you play in your friendships, romantic relationships and family dynamics,' explains Lue. 'You may be the Listener, or the Agony Aunt, or the Fixer, or the Entertainer. Whatever your role, if you do tend to have a very defined "job" when it comes to managing the feelings of the people around you, this can be a tell-tale sign of people-pleasing, as you've most likely learned this behaviour is the best way of feeling needed.' We do tend to fall into different dynamics with friends and family, but if you never feel you can flip the script and, for example, be the one who is listened to or entertained, then you may not be expressing your full self in that relationship.

You have moments of boiling over

'Often, something small can tip us over the edge, because we're like pressure cookers that have been on the hob too long,' says Lue. 'It might happen at work, but often it's with family or friends, and all of our pent-up emotion we've been holding back in the name of keeping others happy suddenly erupts in a seemingly inane moment. If you've experienced burnout, stress-related illness or had an explosion where you've been tipped over the edge by one request or criticism too many, these are clues that you've been suppressing your own needs, desires or opinions. It's like the emotional equivalent of running lots of red lights, ignoring the warning signs and consistently pushing yourself past your own limits and into the danger zone. At some point, you're going to crash.'

You often find yourself in unequal relationships

'If you have a pattern of being with emotionally unavailable or selfish people, romantically or otherwise, that is a sure-fire sign you're a people-pleaser,' says Lue. 'There is a part of you that is drawn to people like this and puts up with them because you're holding on to an underlying belief that if you can just be pleasing enough, they will suddenly transform into a kinder or more emotionally available person.

'What happens is, people-pleasers tend to hold themselves accountable for the way everyone else around them behaves,' she adds. 'This might manifest as false niceties, appeasing and agreeing even when they really don't, and apologising a lot. They might have thoughts like, "If they don't treat me well it's just because I haven't tried hard enough," or "That person is only angry because I did something wrong and provoked them". Ultimately, it's a manifestation of anxiety – that you'll be out of control, that you'll be disliked – and so you try to get ahead of the fear by attempting to anticipate and manage how other people behave.' But that is a futile task, because none of us can control the feelings or actions of others. It's a vicious cycle that leads us nowhere but absolutely exhausts us.

So what can I do to tackle my people-pleasing behaviours?

Observe yourself

'Spend a week observing how you spend your bandwidth,' suggests Lue. 'You could note down all the interactions you have that leave you with some of those people-pleasing feelings of resentment, guilt, anxiety, overwhelm [and] powerlessness and track it that way. Or you could keep a tally of every time you say "yes" to something you wish you hadn't. It could even be as simple as putting ticks down in "yes", "no" and "maybe" columns to see what your most common answers are when someone asks something of you.'

Exercises like these can be eye-opening, because they draw your attention to how often you go through the day leaning in to whatever people ask of you and saying 'yes' before really thinking about the implications. It can also highlight where your people-pleasing shows up most, as sometimes it's very siloed – you might be assertive and in control in the workplace, but tend to roll over in the presence of a parent or partner.

'A common pattern people find is that they frontload their weeks,' explains Lue. 'Say their people-pleasing generally shows up at work; they might feel refreshed by the weekend and dive into Monday saying "yes" all over the shop, so that by Wednesday they feel completely overloaded. Observing your behaviour will help you bring awareness to the areas you need to focus on.'

APPLY IT: *Keep a bank of questions in your arsenal that can help you stall for time when someone asks you for something, giving you more time to fight that entrenched impulse to say 'yes' and truly think about your answer. Before you respond, ask yourself: How much time will this take and do I have that time? Is this something I really want to do? How might taking on this task make me feel? What, realistically, might happen if I say no? Research has proven that taking even a few seconds before making a call can greatly improve your decision-making accuracy.*

Cut your yeses

'See if you can halve the number of times you say "yes" or override your own instincts half the time over the course of a week,' suggests Lue. 'This is where the rubber hits the road. When you start to contemplate saying no to things, and you are forced to think about the reality of what you can actually do as opposed to saying yes and dealing with it later, it *will* bring up anxiety at first – but it will also help you figure out exactly where your people-pleasing is coming from.'

As ever, tracking how you feel is key. If you need to cancel plans with a friend that you'd said 'yes' to knowing full well you wouldn't be able to make it, note down how it feels in the moment. If you decide to maintain your boundaries and say you can't do something for someone, even when you know they'll be disappointed, write down your uncomfortable thoughts. Try speaking up when someone's opinion doesn't sit right with you, and be really honest when you write about what happens next – does the world fall apart, or does everyone move on pretty quickly? Having the facts in front of you after your first experiment with putting your foot down will help you understand that your fears about displeasing others have often been overblown.

APPLY IT: *Self-talk is one of those things that can feel cringeworthy or unnatural at first, but its effects can be powerful. When you feel tempted to cave and say 'yes' to something even though there's some resistance deep down, remind yourself of why boundaries are important with some positive self-talk. Repeat affirmations in the mirror, or write them down if that feels too strange: 'I deserve to have time for myself. I don't owe anyone my time or energy. I don't have to do things that don't make me feel good. I am strong and self-assured and that is a positive thing.'*

Get in touch with your priorities

We are only human, which means we can't devote the same amount of time and energy to everything: working, nurturing our friendships, being there for family, looking after ourselves and pursuing our passions can all be full-time jobs in themselves. The key to turning up that inner voice and getting in touch with what is important to you (and remember, this will fluctuate over the course of your life) is to start setting concrete goals and priorities, week to week or even daily, that will help you channel your energy into the right areas. By proxy, focusing on what matters to you will help you get closer to your own values and opinions, and make you less likely to shapeshift depending on who you're with, so you won't feel the need to assume the opinions and personalities of the people around you.

APPLY IT: *At the start of each week, write down in a diary or in your phone's Notes app – somewhere you'll see it often – what you want to focus on above all else that week. It might be getting ahead on a project at work, meaning you'll have less time for social activities, or making sure you're there for a friend going through a tough time, meaning you won't have the capacity to do an extra favour for a family member this week. The idea is to help you be realistic about your capacity. Concrete priorities give you permission to say no or deprioritise other things, and avoid burning out by trying to keep all your plates spinning at all times.*

Reframe what being a good person means to you

People-pleasers, somewhere along the way, have learned to equate being a 'good' or 'nice' person with being completely selfless – understandable, as it's a link that is made throughout our cultural education, particularly for women and girls. But the truth is, never tending to your own needs leaves you depleted and acting from a place of resentment. Surely it is far better to help others when you have the capacity, and because you truly want to?

As you start to roll back your people-pleasing behaviours and act from a place of authenticity, you'll notice the impact on your relationships, too: namely, the fact that most people don't suddenly see you as a selfish and awful person. You'll form new connections more rooted in mutual respect and shared values, thanks to the fact you're voicing your true opinions.

It is worth noting, though, that some relationships may *not* survive this more empowered, more real version of you. You may have maintained some relationships that were based on the other person taking without ever giving, relying on you to be sacrificial and never challenge them on anything – and though that kind of relationship is never good for us, it can be painful to see it crumble. Try to remember: the people who take issue with you setting boundaries are usually the people who benefitted from you not having any.

APPLY IT: *As a journal prompt, think about two or three people you admire – in your life or from afar – and make a list of the qualities that you feel make them impressive or aspirational people. It sounds simple, but it's a shortcut to understanding that there is often a gulf between the way we think about others and the way we think about ourselves; people-pleasers often respect those who are assertive, go for what they want and give to others from a place of integrity. Those are the qualities we should value and encourage in ourselves, too.*

We need to talk about perfectionism

Ever reached for the 'I'm a perfectionist' line in a job interview when asked what your biggest weakness is, thinking you've gamed the system and managed to make yourself look good? If so, it may be time to think again, because despite the way society has longed portrayed perfectionism as a generally positive affliction, the truth is it can be a very limiting and stressful side effect of people-pleaser syndrome.

By definition, perfectionism is striving for flawlessness and holding yourself to very high standards, whether that be in your work, your appearance or even your hobbies. This is where the waters grow murky, because just like people-pleasing, a lot of the fallout of perfectionism can be positive. It is a motivator, meaning we might be driven to get great marks in school exams or go above and beyond in our jobs, leading to praise and promotions.

But the issue is in the word 'perfect' and the fact that what we are always striving for is an unachievable goal. No matter how hard we work or how talented we are at something, being human means we will always slip up, leave room for improvement or drop the ball sometimes – and that is OK. But unhealthy perfectionists stay on this treadmill of chasing flawlessness forever, never quite reaching the destination they're trying to get to. That's an exhausting existence that can lead to feelings of failure and low self-esteem, despite the fact we're excelling. It's a painful irony, especially because we generally apply this pressure to ourselves.

The perfectionism masterclass:
Healthy vs unhealthy perfectionism
by Katherine Schafler

Katherine Schafler has spent years observing and studying perfectionism in her capacity as a psychotherapist running her own private practice on New York City's Wall Street and working as an onsite therapist at Google HQ, culminating in her best-selling book The Perfectionist's Guide To Losing Control. *Here, she illustrates the difference between healthy and unhealthy – or maladaptive – perfectionism.*

'Maladaptive perfectionism is the kind that often manifests as a response to trauma, neglect or abuse in childhood – however severe. This is the kind that can be harmful, but not all perfectionism is terrible and it's important to not assume there is something "wrong" with you, whatever your perfectionism looks like. It's just a reaction to your environment.

'There are two guiding questions to consider here: *how* am I striving and *why* am I striving? The "how" involves asking yourself, am I striving in a way that is burning me out, restraining my relationships or threatening my wellbeing? Or am I striving in a way that's making me feel more alive, more curious? Sure, I get tired sometimes and my work is hard, even stressful, but overall I feel like I'm being more myself. The latter is the healthy version.

'And the "why" is about what's driving you to strive towards this goal of perfection. Am I striving towards this goal because I think that it's going to certify my belonging in a certain group – after I get this degree or after I get this job title, then I can call myself a success? After I lose this weight and do this to my hair, then I can call myself pretty? After my child performs this task perfectly, then I can call myself a good mother? Or am I striving because I already know that I'm successful, I already know that I'm beautiful. I already know that I have so much to give, and I just want to keep expressing that and celebrating that with the world around me? That is where healthy perfectionism is coming from.

'One example I often use is people who are striving to make themselves look good, physically. One person, who is healthy, wants to look their best because it makes them feel good and they want to reflect externally how they feel on the inside. The person who is not approaching it from a healthy place wants to look good because they already feel like they're walking into the room at a deficit, and so they need to do everything they can think of to compensate for that. It's almost like an armour.'

Signs you might be an unhealthy perfectionist

You're not able to walk away from a task until you feel it's perfect or as close as possible

For perfectionists, 'good enough' is not an option. This is not an inherently negative thing, but when exercised to a punishing degree it can be overwhelming. It is often rooted in the belief that, say, turning in a piece of work or presenting a meal to guests that's simply fine is a reflection of who you are as a person – that you're only as impressive and worthy as the last thing you did.

You procrastinate a lot

The flipside of this is procrastination, a very common symptom of perfectionism. We can get disheartened by what we see as our own lack of ability mid-task, and the enormity of the goal we've set ourselves. We can also spend a lot of time editing, second-guessing, going over things with a fine-tooth comb and generally putting off the end of a task, for fear it will not be perfect.

You're unwilling to try something new unless you're sure you can do it well

The pressure of needing a piece of work to be perfect can make it difficult to even start in the first place. In our subconscious minds, not doing something at all is better than doing it badly, and often we'll beat ourselves up for not being good at something even if we've never done it before. Which leads on to our next point . . .

You can be very self-critical

Perfectionists tend to have a harsh inner critic: less encouraging, more drill sergeant. Do you find you beat yourself up over small mistakes, dub yourself 'stupid' or 'incapable' for not nailing things first time and generally talk to yourself in a way you never would your loved ones? It may be the perfectionism talking, meaning it's time to cut yourself some slack.

You find it difficult to be happy for others

This is the less flattering – and less talked-about – element of perfectionism, and it's rooted in comparison. When we see others achieving a lot, we can struggle to celebrate their wins without seeing it as a reflection of our own failures and shortcomings. Perfectionism often heightens feelings of competition and

inadequacy because it's rooted in needing to prove ourselves
all the time.

How to break out of harmful perfectionist habits

Try zooming out

When you can feel yourself getting caught up in tiny details or
labouring over a task that shouldn't take long, it's helpful to step away
and consider the bigger picture. Ask yourself whether expending this
much time and effort on one thing will have that much of an impact on
the end result – will making the presentation look perfect really impact
the way the client receives your pitch? This will help you reprioritise
and keep momentum rather than getting stuck.

Tick the boxes

Often, perfectionism can feel like an endless slog with no goal in
sight – nothing is ever truly 'done' because it's never truly perfect. For
more daunting tasks, it's worth writing yourself a checklist of small
goals that will lead you to the finish line, that you can tick off as you
go. Once you're at the end of that list, you're done – no more
finessing needed.

Lower the stakes

When we're striving to make everything ten out of ten, sometimes we
build up the importance of things in our heads: our friend's surprise
birthday must be the best party they've ever had, or the report we're
writing for our boss has to completely blow them away. But the people
around us aren't expecting us to excel at everything, all the time, and
a perfectionist's standards are generally high above everyone else's –
what you think is an average party or report, for example, the people

around you will most likely see as excellent. Be realistic about how your own output compares to that of other people, and you'll realise you're doing just fine.

Rip off the plaster

Often, the fear of being imperfect builds up because we rarely allow ourselves to see what happens when we are – there's little evidence to show that everything won't fall apart, right? A powerful way to shift your mindset is to experiment with imperfectionism. You could consciously do something to an average level, not giving it the full effort you usually do, or try something brand new that you can do badly without anyone needing to see it – say, painting or writing a poem. Observe how you feel and what happens next. Chances are it will challenge your core belief that the balance of your life hinges on being good at everything.

3. Why boundaries aren't about other people

If one word has burst through the glut of 'therapy speak' that's recently entered the mainstream lexicon, it is 'boundaries'. It is not a new concept; one of its earliest uses in the context of wellbeing appears in a 1989 self-help book called *Tired of Trying to Measure Up* by motivational speaker Jeff VanVonderen, who wrote: 'Personal boundaries notify others that you have the right to have your own opinion, feel your own feelings, and protect the privacy of your own physical being.'

It's a concept most of us could use in some areas of our lives, a way to clarify and set down what we will and won't accept from others in order to be the best versions of ourselves. A boundary can be vocal, something you explicitly say to a family member, partner, friend or colleague to make clear what you need, or it could be something you hold in your own head as a reminder. It might be a boundary around your time; say you've got a friend who expects replies to their lengthy, emotionally intense messages at all hours of the day, you may want to impose a boundary around when and how you're able to respond. It might be a boundary around the way a colleague speaks to you, for example if you find their gossiping or inappropriate jokes uncomfortable.

The thing is, although they're useful – if not crucial – in a world where it seems there are endless demands on our time and attention and less and less space for us to vocalise our needs, boundaries can easily be abused or misconstrued. This is an issue that Melissa Urban, CEO and author, has unpacked in her best-seller *The Book of Boundaries*.

'There are two common misconceptions when it comes to boundaries,' explains Urban. 'The first is that boundaries are about telling other people what to do. That's not at all true. Boundaries don't tell other people what to do, they tell others the actions that you are willing to take to keep yourself safe and healthy, and to preserve the relationship. A real boundary is always within your power and control, and you should always be able to hold it to preserve your own mental health, time, energy or space – regardless of how the other person reacts.

'The second misconception is that boundaries are selfish (or cold, or controlling, or any other term most often associated with a woman who expresses a need),' adds Urban. 'Boundaries are a kindness to yourself and to your relationship. Boundaries are how you ensure the relationship feels good to both people, and how the people who care about you know how to engage with you in a way that feels safe and healthy.'

In fact, Urban explains, not being clear about what you need in a relationship is not accommodating, it's harmful. 'In most situations, not sharing a boundary is actually the *least* kind thing you can do. Yes, it bothers you when your mother-in-law shows up without calling, but you don't say anything, because you're trying to be nice. Except every time she shows up at your front door, you're short, impatient, irritated and distracted. Now she's wondering what she did to upset you, and your relationship (not to mention everyone else in the house) is suffering. Boundaries are how we ensure trust, respect, and good feelings in a relationship – and often, they're the only thing that allows us to preserve them.'

How do I know if need to set a boundary?

There are a few signs that your life is lacking in boundaries and you would benefit from putting some in place. An obvious one is that you feel burned out, meaning you're expending more energy – mentally or physically – than you truly have to give. Another giveaway is that you feel resentful towards something or someone; this might be because they're repeatedly overstepping and demanding too much of you, or because a part of you wishes you could say no in the way they do. If you're lacking in boundaries, you may also feel that people often take advantage of you, aren't receptive to your needs or don't do as much for you as you do for them.

The seven types of boundary we're all entitled to set

Emotional

These boundaries can be the trickiest to maintain as they are generally required in our closest relationships, but they can be really important to your wellbeing. An emotional boundary may mean telling a loved one you don't have the bandwidth to work through their trauma or take on their emotional burdens, or it might mean not engaging in conversations about political, heavy or triggering topics when you don't want to.

Physical

This is about who you feel comfortable touching you, having in your personal space, and commenting on your body and physical appearance. It can also apply to what you put *into* your body; for example, a subtle violation of this boundary may be someone pressuring you to drink alcohol after you've stated you don't want to.

Mental

Mental boundaries tend to be more inward-looking; they're about allowing yourself to have your own personal thoughts, beliefs and opinions, and being OK with other people not agreeing with them. Issues around mental boundaries can crop up if you have people-pleasing tendencies, as you might feel inclined to go along with what others say. Keeping a phrase like 'We don't need to agree' in your arsenal can be helpful.

Financial

Money can be a fraught topic in our relationships, and we all have different values, priorities and needs when it comes to spending and saving. Being explicit about yours – whether it's a birthday or hen do you don't want to shell out for, or a friend asking for a loan you don't feel comfortable giving – might feel hard in the moment but is vital for both yourself and the health of the relationship.

Time

If you're the kind of person that gets sucked in to helping out a friend before realising you've no time left to work on yourself, you may need better boundaries around time. You may also need these boundaries when it comes to people in your life who are always late to meet up with you, or people who expect you to answer your phone whenever they call.

Communication

Boundaries around communication could involve raising an issue with the way someone is speaking to you, asking for a level of privacy or protecting your right to not respond to a message or email until you are ready to.

Energy

Like your time, your energy is finite, and you should make sure you're protecting it. Setting boundaries around energy is about not spending too much time with people whom you find draining or who negatively impact your mood, creating protected time to rest and revive.

How to set a boundary

Step 1

'The first step in setting a boundary is knowing you need one,' says Urban. 'Often, we feel this general sense of dread, anxiety, avoidance or resentment when we think of, see, or hear from a certain person. But we don't immediately recognise that those feelings stem from a limit (or twelve) that this person has been overrunning. Use those feelings – dread, anxiety, avoidance or resentment – as your first red flag that a boundary is needed.'

Step 2

'Next,' Urban continues, 'you'll have to identify the specific boundary that will bring the most relief. If there are multiple boundaries, start with one. In these situations, we often feel the urge to leave, hang up, or blow up, but there is a more specific issue at play besides "I hate how I feel right now". Dig a little deeper into the "why" of your resentment or anxiety. Is it because this person is always offering unsolicited opinions, or over-parents you with your own kids, or is constantly dismissing your feelings? Choose one specific scenario where, if it just didn't happen again, it would bring you great relief. That's the first boundary you set.'

Step 3

'Finally, you need to actually set the boundary, using clear, kind words,' says Urban. 'You can't hint, be passive-aggressive or vague. They can't read your mind. Create a short script that outlines the need or feeling you want to address. "Oh, let me stop you there – I'm not looking for advice here, I was just sharing. If you're not in a place to just listen, I'll change the subject." Then practise that script until it feels natural and comfortable, and so you don't water it down with "I'm sorry, but . . ." or ". . . if that's OK with you".'

A note on guilt

'Guilt is a social, moral emotion that promotes relationship repair and encourages us to connect with, care for, and help one another,' explains Urban. 'When we do something legitimately wrong – something that hurts our family or community – we feel bad, and that helps to remind us not to do that thing again. But the guilt that comes along with setting a boundary is unearned guilt. We haven't done anything wrong, so there is nothing to feel bad about.

'Many people on the receiving end of a boundary want you to feel guilty. They'll try to pressure you, guilt-trip you, or manipulate you into feeling bad. They'll paint you as the bad guy, the one with "all the rules", the difficult one, because then you might abandon this inconvenient (for them) boundary altogether.

'If guilt comes knocking after you've set a boundary (or if someone tries to guilt-trip you), remind yourself, "I've done nothing wrong. I deserve to have my needs met. My comfort and feelings matter just as much as theirs. I've shared my boundary clearly and kindly, and how they choose to receive it is not my responsibility."'

How to respect other people's boundaries

Chances are you innately understand and respect when the people in your life lay down their own boundaries around their time, space and resources, but it can be beneficial to keep the below tips front of mind when tensions arise or you're struggling to understand why someone is behaving differently. Showing you care about the comfort and wellbeing of the people in your life is also a sure-fire way to strengthen your relationships – and often you can lend a helping hand in them setting the boundaries they need.

Stay curious

Checking in with friends and family about what they need and whether something is OK to do or say around them is a lovely way to let them know you respect their boundaries, and empowers them to speak up if they're finding boundaries hard to set. It doesn't have to be a big deal; a simple 'Is it OK if I do this?' goes a long way. It's also valuable to try to learn and understand others' experiences of the world and how that might impact what they're comfortable with, based on their gender, culture or sexuality, for example.

Acknowledge what you hear

If someone states what they need from you or your relationship, it's often worth repeating it back to reassure them you've taken it on board and check you've understood it correctly. It's an easy way to avoid any misunderstanding or resentment down the line.

Apologise when you need to

If you cross a line with someone, even if you didn't know it was there, it's always worthwhile to apologise and take responsibility. It's in this way that we can often get into valuable and open conversations with our loved ones and tighten our bonds – mistakes are there to learn from, so don't judge yourself harshly if you accidentally violate someone's boundaries.

Journal prompts for boundary-setting

Use these journal prompts to explore where and why you may need to set some boundaries in your life, being as honest with yourself as possible. Remember, it's not a failure, but an opportunity to create some healthier parameters that both your mental health and your relationships will benefit from.

- *What are your three non-negotiables in a romantic relationship?*
- *What are your three non-negotiables in a friendship?*
- *What is one thing you wish you did more of?*
- *What is one thing you wish you did less of?*
- *What is one thing other people do that saps your energy?*
- *What are the warning signs that someone has breached your boundary?*
- *How can you communicate what you need better?*

4. What's your attachment style?

Discovering what our attachment style is has become increasingly popular in recent years, as more of us seek deeper and more meaningful ways to understand our relationships with other people. Attachment styles are a way of defining the manner in which we tend to approach and navigate our romantic relationships, and they're generally based on the formative connections we experienced growing up.

There are four different types of attachment styles, which can all give insights into why we might fall into certain behavioural patterns when it comes to dating or finding love, whether we're the type to throw ourselves into a new connection or hold something back until we're sure it's reciprocated. However, while simply identifying our attachment style can be useful and shed light on why we behave the way we do, it's important to understand it fully so it doesn't get in the way of forming healthy bonds with other people.

'An attachment style is literally a relational blueprint,' says Dr Sophie Mort, better known as Dr Soph, a clinical psychologist and the author of *A Manual for Being Human* and *(Un)stuck*. 'The bonds that we have early in life with our caregivers and the people around us earliest on form a blueprint of how we understand relationships going forward.

'Attachment styles define what you expect other people to do in response to you; how you expect them to treat you and how you stay emotionally safe and connected in your relationship,' Dr Soph continues. 'Your attachment style often really only affects you in quite intimate or anxiety-provoking scenarios, and dating tends to be the relationship that is most intimate and causes the most stress, so this is where attachment styles are most relevant.'

You don't necessarily need to psychoanalyse yourself or your family in order to understand what attachment style you are and why. All you need to do is identify which one you relate to and understand what you can do to make sure it supports, rather than negatively impacts, your relationships. Here's Dr Soph's guide to figuring out what your attachment style is and managing it so you can get the best out of your relationships.

What are the different attachment styles?

Secure
'This is the attachment style I think most people wish they had, and roughly fifty per cent of the population does have a secure attachment style,' says Dr Soph. She explains that people develop this attachment style when they have caregivers or people around them early on in life that meet their emotional needs. 'Someone with a secure attachment style generally doesn't feel anxious in a new relationship. They tend to believe they are deserving of love and affection and that they can trust others to be there for them,' explains Dr Soph.

Signs you may have a secure attachment style:

- You tend to believe you'll be accepted by others.
- You don't mind being alone.
- You feel able to make mistakes from time to time.
- You're empathetic and good at relating to others.
- You're not afraid of commitment.

Avoidant

'Avoidant attachment styles describe someone who learned early on that at least one person in their life consistently missed their needs. They learned that if they expressed their emotional needs people won't be there for them,' Dr Soph says. 'An avoidant person will absolutely want to connect with people, but should people get emotionally close to them, their brain protects them from a fear that the person won't be there for them by shutting down and holding that person at arm's length.'

Signs you may have an avoidant attachment style:

- You don't open up or show your emotions easily.
- In times of stress or upset, you'd rather be alone.
- You struggle with intimacy.
- You place a big emphasis on being independent.
- You often find romantic partners clingy or demanding.

Anxious

'Someone with an anxious attachment style has learned early on that people would intermittently be there for them. For example, a caregiver might have been absolutely attuned with their needs at one moment, but then have disappeared the next moment, or required the child to be their emotional support crutch in a way that was overwhelming,' Dr Soph explains.

'These adults start initiating contact as often as possible, knowing that at some point they'll get what they need. They might call themselves needy because when the new seeds of a relationship form, they're excited and give it attention. As the other person moves away, they give the relationship even more attention.'

Signs you may have an anxious attachment style:

- You don't feel comfortable being alone.
- You struggle to trust others.
- You need plenty of validation from a partner.
- You have a tendency to be jealous.
- You struggle to say 'no' in relationships.

Disorganised

'The disorganised attachment style develops because a child tried both the avoidant and anxious attachment style and neither worked,' Dr Soph says. 'This person might crave attention but be absolutely terrified of it happening, so they put up walls.'

Signs you may have a disorganised attachment style:

- Your relationships tend to be unpredictable.
- You have a strong fear of rejection.
- You desire closeness but push people away.
- You sometimes feel unlovable.
- You have a negative self-image.

The attachment style quiz: which one most applies to you?

Dr Soph recommends asking yourself the following questions to find out which attachment style you're most aligned with.

1. Do you believe people, particularly the people you date, can be there for you and support you in a way that feels good?
   A) Yes
   B) No
   C) Sometimes

2. Do you often feel attracted to people you meet?
   A) Sometimes
   B) I rarely ever find people I am attracted to
   C) Often, I have high hopes for many people

3. When people get emotionally close to you, do you shut down and pull away or do you lean in offering more and more attention?
   A) Neither – I like to go with the flow and keep things steady
   B) I mostly shut down and pull away
   C) Leaning in is my thing

4. Are you self-reliant or do you usually put your partner's needs first?
   A) Neither – it's give and take
   B) I rely on myself and no one else
   C) It's all about them – if they need something, I can meet that need

5. Have you ever been told you are needy or cold while dating?
   A) Neither
   B) High walls and cold as ice
   C) People always say I am needy and, even when they don't say it,
      I believe they are thinking it

If you mostly answered As, you probably have a secure attachment style.
If you mostly answered Bs, you probably have an avoidant attachment style.
If you mostly answered Cs, you probably have an anxious attachment style.

If your answers were a fairly even mix of Bs and Cs, you probably have a disorganised attachment style.

So how do I manage my attachment style?

Firstly, know that you are normal

'Stop beating yourself up if you feel like there's something wrong with you,' Dr Soph advises. 'Often, people with anxious attachment styles feel embarrassed or that there's something wrong with them, but the reason you feel the way you do is because you were very good at adapting as a child. There is no right or wrong, just the way our early life has shaped us. Understanding this is a huge step towards having the kind of relationships we really want.'

Think about people you know in secure relationships

'Write a list of friends, colleagues or family members who seem like they're in a secure relationship. Think about the specific things they've said or done which make you and others feel calm and safe around them and write down a concrete set of actions you can take,' Dr Soph advises. 'Think about the techniques you've developed as part of your attachment style and the things other people do instead,' she adds.

Learn to communicate your needs

'With an anxious attachment style, to feel safe and secure you might simply need to know that the other person cares about you, so learn to communicate that need,' Dr Soph says. 'If you need someone to text you more, tell them you need them to text you more. If you have an avoidant attachment style, you need to communicate how you feel and tell people how they can help you with this,' she continues. 'For example, say something like: "I can feel quite overwhelmed when I feel emotionally close to someone. Sometimes, I just need a few days on my own to reset."'

Seek out securely attached people

'Insecurely attached people tend to gravitate towards each other. So, often an anxiously attached person will find an avoidantly attached person,' says Dr Soph. 'It feels great at first but it becomes a vicious circle where the avoidant person is totally shut down and the anxious person is really overwhelmed. If you're in this anxious-avoidant cycle, it's crucial to get good at communicating to find a way that works for the two of you,' she advises. 'Or seek out securely attached people with whom you won't end up in this cycle.'

Do an attachment style quiz with any new partners

'I've seen a lot of people doing attachment style quizzes together when they start dating, which can be so helpful when it comes to setting boundaries and building good communication in a relationship,' says Dr Soph. 'However, attachment styles are not fixed, so if you have an avoidant attachment style but you date someone who has an attachment style that is even more avoidant than yours, you might start to develop an anxious attachment style,' she explains. 'It's useful to know your attachment style, but it's even more important to recognise when it's changing so you know how to communicate with your partner accordingly.'

Don't worry if you feel your attachment style kicking in

'Even if you've managed to override your attachment style, your brain will still use it as a coping skill during times of distress,' Dr Soph says. 'On occasion, these old ways will come up, but that only has to be temporary, so long as when you notice them coming up, you start to practise the healthier communication techniques you've learned.'

The break-up masterclass: Breaking up is hard to do, but this will make it easier

by Stephanie Ambrosius

Sometimes, two people's attachment styles just don't mesh, and you might realise a relationship has come to its natural end. You're probably used to hearing about break-ups from the perspective of the person who has been broken up with. Of course, that rarely feels like a good position to be in, as it often causes heartbreak, disappointment and resentment. But being the person who is breaking up with someone can also be a difficult and painful experience. The guilt that comes with inflicting heartbreak on someone else can feel debilitating, as can making the decision to break up with a romantic partner you care about.

Ending a relationship is a personal experience, but it's also one in which you're probably having to prioritise someone else's feelings. You might have spent weeks, months or even years contemplating whether breaking up with someone is the right thing to do. Figuring out what you're going to say to them and then navigating that post-romantic relationship can also be time-consuming.

'Just because a relationship has ended, that doesn't mean it wasn't successful,' says Stephanie Ambrosius, a relationship therapist who uses cognitive behavioural therapy (CBT) methods to help individuals and couples deal with various issues. 'I help a lot of couples who have to stay in touch after a break-up,' Ambrosius says, explaining that many of her clients are bringing up their children together or have other commitments that mean they have to try to maintain a positive relationship.

But even if there is nothing tying you and your ex together after a break-up, making the process as pain-free as possible for both of you is still a good idea. Here, Ambrosius shares her advice on how to do so, from deciding whether a break-up is the right thing for you, to navigating that difficult conversation and maintaining a healthy post-romantic relationship.

How to decide whether to break up with a romantic partner

Ultimately, the decision to put an end to a relationship is extremely personal, but there are some things an expert like Ambrosius suggests you consider if you're having doubts. It's worth noting that the following advice will be most relevant for people who've been in a long-term relationship rather than something that's fairly new – and it is aimed at those in a safe relationship who feel able to voice their feelings and exercise their autonomy without threat. If you feel you are in a relationship that's controlling, abusive or coercive, you can contact Refuge's national domestic abuse helpline 24 hours a day on 0808 2000 247. If you feel you are in immediate danger, always call 999.

Figure out the real reason you want to break up with your partner and find out if it's the right one

'Before you break up with your partner, take some time to think about whether it's definitely the right decision,' Ambrosius advises. She explains that there are often other factors affecting people's decisions to break up with their partners that can blur their judgement. They include:

- external pressures, like friends and family's opinions of your partner
- fear of commitment – maybe you have an avoidant attachment style
- trust issues, often because of negative past relationships

If you are facing any of these issues, they might be things you can work through together with your partner. If you're not facing any of these issues, and you're still unsure if breaking up is the right thing to do, Ambrosius recommends considering the following questions:

- Are you happy in this relationship?
- Do you feel fulfilled in this relationship?
- Are you happy with who you are when you're with your partner?
- Is the relationship still romantic?

If you're answering 'no' to some or all of these questions, it may be grounds to consider the future of your relationship.

Don't decide that it's over on your own
Ambrosius does stress that you should have some conversations with your partner before you actually break up with them. This will allow you to work together to see if there is a way to save your relationship. 'They might be thinking the same thing, or they might not know you're feeling this way and there might be a lot of things you can change to get your relationship back on track,' Ambrosius says. Only you will know if the issues are too significant to work through.

How to plan for your break-up

Timing is key, but don't look for excuses to delay it

'I think it can be beneficial to wait for the right time to break
up with someone,' Ambrosius says. 'Consider what's
going on in your partner's life and be compassionate.' She
explains that it might be worth delaying a break-up if your
partner is going through a challenging personal
experience, like having difficulties at work or grieving
a family member.

'But don't leave it for too long or use birthdays, holidays or
events you have planned as an excuse to delay breaking up,'
Ambrosius adds. 'I've seen people who have stayed together for
years because they never found the "right" moment to break up.'
There will probably never be a perfect moment to break up with
someone, Ambrosius advises, so have some perspective when it
comes to putting it off.

Choose a comfortable space

'If you feel safe with the person you're breaking up with, [doing
it] at home in a quiet space is probably the best place to have a
difficult conversation like this one,' Ambrosius advises. 'It's best
to do it where other people won't be able to hear and so can't
get involved – definitely avoid clubs, pubs and restaurants and
make sure neither of you are intoxicated.'

Ambrosius says that breaking up with someone over the
phone is not a good idea. Phone calls should be a last resort –
for example, if you don't feel safe with the person or you won't
be able to meet them in person in the near future. And she
stresses that you should never break up with someone via text

message. Not only can texts be misinterpreted but they don't offer real closure.

What to say when you're breaking up with your partner

Position things from your perspective and stick to the facts

'Transparency is good when it comes to breaking up with someone, but try to avoid making the other person feel bad. Always speak from your perspective,' Ambrosius advises, adding that you should try to start your sentences with 'I' rather than 'you'. Rather than saying, 'You never want to spend time with me', try 'I'm not satisfied with the amount of time we spend together.'

'Never perceive intentions,' she adds. 'Stick to the facts that the other person can reflect on.' You should also offer the other person a chance to speak, Ambrosius advises, adding, 'Try not to ambush them.'

Find the balance when it comes to being kind and offering sympathy

'You want to feel like a good person after your break-up and you want the other person to feel as good as is possible too,' Ambrosius says. 'Listen to what they have to say and stay calm, because you can't control their response. You can offer them sympathy, but don't go back on what you've said because of their reaction if this is truly what you want.' From this point, it's crucial to set boundaries. 'You need them to know that while you can offer them support, there's no going back on the break-up,' Ambrosius says.

How to have a positive experience after your break-up

Take some space away from each other

Space and time are, famously, what heal a broken heart, and Ambrosius confirms that taking space from your ex is crucial in allowing you both closure. 'You can be there for them sometimes, but only if you have boundaries in place so you don't come to rely on each other,' she says. Part of the boundaries you put in place should focus on preventing intimate contact. 'Avoid break-up sex,' Ambrosius says.

And make sure that you've got supportive people around you whom you can speak to. You're probably used to going to your partner for support, so having someone else there can help you successfully take the space from them you need.

'You have to own your emotion and they have to own theirs as well – they're an adult and they will get through it,' Ambrosius says, adding that if you are seriously concerned, you could ask a mutual friend to check in on your ex. 'But, ultimately, checking on them won't be your job anymore, so there's only so long you can do this for,' she adds.

Let any kind of friendship form organically

'It's too hard for many people to be friends with their exes, particularly when they start to date someone else,' Ambrosius says. 'If a friendship is going to happen, it will be gradual and organic. Right at the beginning of the break-up, you can't expect to be friends – you have to live without that person for a while because you can't rely on them anymore.'

If you are going to become friends, Ambrosius explains, 'you will gravitate back towards each other when the time is right'.

Reaching out at a later date when you both might have achieved a certain amount of closure can be a good idea. 'Your ex might not want to be friends and that's a risk that you have to be willing to take when you break up with them. But if you set healthy boundaries right away, you'll have a better chance of a successful friendship,' Ambrosius says.

━━━━━━━

WORK

5. The shifting shape of ambition

'What do you want to be when you grow up?'

It's one of the first questions we're asked as children, planting the seed early that who we are and what we do are closely intertwined. As adults, it's the first thing we want to know about each other: what's your job and do you enjoy it? It makes sense, considering just how much time most of us spend at work – thirty-five hours per week, on average – but it's also a symptom of a world in which the lines between success in life and success in our careers are blurred. Not until recently have the vast majority of us considered there might be a difference.

Think about what the archetypal successful, ambitious person looks like in your mind's eye. Perhaps you picture someone in a sharp suit presenting to a boardroom, or sitting in their corner office tapping away at a computer late into the night. Someone who spends their spare time reading books about productivity and listening to podcasts sharing the secrets of CEOs while they ferret away on their side hustles. Though the word ambition simply means 'desire to achieve success', our collective idea of what that success looks like tends to be fairly narrow. For so long, it has meant the pursuit of money and power, climbing the ranks and putting your career above all else.

Many of us came of age in the era of 'girlbosses' and 'She-EOs', optimised morning routines and five-year plans, all hammering home the idea that to graft day and night towards your career goals – often at the expense of your wellbeing – was virtuous, admirable, *feminist*, even. In a way, it was: no other generation of women had come so close to equal opportunity in the workplace or had so many options available to them when it came to making a living. The glass ceiling was just waiting to be smashed, we were told, if only we wanted it badly enough. And so we entered the workforce with a blazing ambition to reach the highest heights of our respective careers.

That was, until the flame began to fizzle out, with the final blow dealt by a global pandemic. The word 'burnout' was becoming everyday parlance, and women began to feel like they'd been duped, like the promised rewards of hustle culture had not only failed to materialise, but now seemed further away than ever. Was it all worth it? In a world-shifting period that brought the unpredictability and brevity of life into sharp focus, the answer, for many, was 'not really'.

The past few years have marked a historic turning point in our collective relationship with ambition, the likes of which we haven't seen since the five-day working week was implemented a century ago. To understand how we got here, let's take a closer look at how our relationship with work has evolved over the past century . . .

From homemaking to hustle culture: a brief history of women and work

1940s–1950s

During the Second World War, many women in Britain got their first experience of full-time work, filling the gaps at factories, farms and offices as well as assisting in the war effort and on the front line. How were they thanked for keeping the country afloat? By being largely ousted from their jobs as men returned from the front, and expected to return to the domestic sphere. A baby boom soon followed, and so even those who'd held on to their jobs were forced to abandon them if they were married or had families to care for. A 'marriage bar' was common in many industries in the UK right up until the 1960s, meaning married women were not allowed to work, and statutory maternity leave wouldn't exist until 1975.

1960s–1970s

In 1961, the contraceptive pill was introduced for married women (it would be made available to single women in 1967), and with it came choice. Young women were given the opportunity to prevent or delay having children and access life paths that had previously been reserved for men. There was a spike in the number of jobs available due to a post-war economic boom, and by 1962 there were more than 26,000 women enrolled at universities. This access to education – coupled with the fact that female students often lived away from home and had some financial independence – meant a select group were able to broaden their career aspirations, helped along by the rise of feminist organisations such as the Women's Liberation Movement.

1980s

The yuppie (young, urban professional) lifestyle became aspirational, with a 'work hard to get ahead' ethos spreading among young women who connected big cities and high-flying careers with greater freedom. As the Equal Pay Act of 1970 began to have real-world impact, more women were empowered to take up senior roles. For the first time, employment and identity became intertwined, with 'career women' represented extensively in pop culture. Think 1988 film *Working Girl*, starring Melanie Griffith as a vengeful secretary; Yves Saint Laurent's iconic Rive Gauche advert, which sold perfume to shoulder-padded executives; and *Cosmopolitan* editor Helen Gurley Brown's hit book

Having It All, which encouraged women to graft hard to get whatever they wanted in life.

1990s–2000s

By 1998, Britain had the longest average working week in Europe, and presenteeism bred a new kind of career ladder. Promotions were no longer just about how hard you worked, but how long you stayed in the office. Female employees experienced this culture shift most profoundly, with a fifty-two per cent increase in the number of women expected to work forty-eight-hour weeks between 1992 and 2005. On top of this, a tech revolution meant workers were increasingly plugged in to their jobs. The first ever smartphone was invented by IBM in 1994, and by the early 2000s the BlackBerry reigned supreme. In 2007, Apple changed the game: the iPhone gave users easy access to the internet, emails, spreadsheets – you name it – just as they would have on a computer, but anywhere, at any time. Soon it was nigh-on impossible to leave work at the office door.

Early 2010s

If the 2000s were the beginnings of grind culture, then the 2010s were its heyday. When Sheryl Sandberg, Facebook's first female board member, released her best-selling book *Lean In* in 2013, she told women that they could achieve anything if they just worked hard enough. A year later, Sophia Amoruso, founder of fashion retailer Nasty Gal, published *#Girlboss*, touted as an up-to-date guide to workplace empowerment. These became the 'It' books of the decade, spawning a generation of women striding through Tube stations simultaneously reading career manuals and dictating work emails while sipping kale smoothies. Sandberg and Amoruso led a movement framing corporate success as the pinnacle of feminism, but tellingly, the vast majority of self-titled #girlbosses were white and wealthy. However, women of all backgrounds did find their stories motivating for a time. While historically, women had accounted for a quarter of business owners, that number increased between 2008 and 2016, with fifty-eight per cent of the newly self-employed being female. Feminism and capitalism became intertwined, busyness was a badge of honour and 'being a boss' was as aspirational as avo toast.

Late 2010s

By the end of the 2010s, one in four people in the UK had taken on a side hustle to complement their primary stream of income. Whereas once, few people chose to work an extra job unless out of financial necessity, many now saw side hustles as a creative outlet and a way to accrue cultural cachet. On average, women with additional jobs or businesses worked between six and fifteen extra hours a week, with everything from baking to freelance writing on the agenda. The cultural conversation valued productivity and time-optimisation above all else, with motivational infographics flooding social media and imploring us to make the most of not just our nine-to-five but also our five-to-nine. However, criticisms of the 'cult of busy' were beginning to creep in. By the end of the decade, the World Health Organization had recognised 'workplace burnout' as an occupational phenomenon.

2020s

As concerns grew that our 'always on' culture and obsession with productivity were leading to burnout, March 2020 quickly burst the bubble of life as we knew it. Lockdowns forced us all to slow down, as many jobs went remote and everything else in life was put on hold. At first, home working promised more free time and greater flexibility, but in practice, the boundaries between work and home blurred more than ever. Women were still shouldering the majority of the caring and domestic responsibilities: according to the Institute of Fiscal Studies, mothers were doing an extra one and a half hours of childcare and an additional forty minutes of housework each day compared to their male counterparts. Of parents who were in paid work prior to the pandemic, mothers were one and a half times more likely than fathers to have lost or quit their jobs during lockdown. The result? Unprecedented levels of overwhelm and burnout, with 822,000 workers reporting work-related stress, depression or anxiety.

As life crashed down around us, many women took the opportunity to step off the proverbial treadmill and re-evaluate what was truly important, prompting campaigns such as Flex Appeal to demand flexible working for all. Ultimately, this moment of reflection on the role of work in our lives led to the Great Resignation, which saw one in four people plan to quit their jobs. The shape of ambition was clearly shifting: in a *Stylist* survey from early 2021, seventy-seven per cent of women said their attitude to work had changed over the past year, and a massive seventy-five per cent said they'd like to work fewer days and focus more on their personal lives.

*

The Great Resignation and its fallout wasn't a rejection of ambition itself. Rather, it was a reckoning with what was and wasn't working in the world of work: a wholesale re-examination of the role our jobs played in our lives and identities. In a Women and Work survey of 1,000 people conducted by *Stylist* post-pandemic, more than eighty-one per cent said they were now focused on creating a better work–life balance, and just four in ten said their major life ambitions were linked to work: travelling, having a family and having new experiences all came up trumps. Amid these shifting sands, it's been up to each of us to figure out what exactly we are ambitious *for* in this brave new world – but reframing the way you look at success can take some soul-searching.

 The ambition masterclass:
How to find it, nurture it and keep it
by Sarah Ellis

Sarah Ellis held leadership roles at Barclays and Sainsbury's before co-founding Amazing If, an award-winning career-coaching company. Now, with a top careers podcast and two best-selling books under her belt, she's a leading expert with a refreshing approach to work and the way it fits into a happy, fulfilled life. Step into her office . . .

1. Ambition isn't all about boardrooms and briefcases
'For a very long time, probably right up until the pandemic, it felt like everyone had to have the same, shared version of ambition. Ambition equalled seniority, a fancy job title, constantly chasing promotions and working your way up the ranks of an organisation or career path. The message was, if you're not trying to climb the ladder, what are you doing? You're clearly not ambitious enough. But there are so many problems with that traditional view of ambition.

'Firstly, it implies that we all want to do the same thing in exactly the same way – that we are all the same. A ladder is about following in other people's footsteps, and its legacy is that we see ambition as this very linear and predictable progression. But this framework for what a "successful" career looks like was created a hundred years ago, as a way to put structures into organisations that were mostly employing middle-class, white men. It was never *meant* to help us work better, so it's time to let go of the idea that the only career step worth taking is one that goes up.

'One of my most ambitious moves actually involved working less. When I was in a leadership role at Sainsbury's, I asked if I could go down to four days a week – something that was unheard of at the time unless you had children. But I felt like I needed some space and time to do some more personal development. I was really interested in philosophy and wanted to do some learning around that, and I was in the fortunate position where I could sacrifice twenty per cent of my salary in order to do so. It might not be how we typically think about ambition, but it felt like a really ambitious ask at the time, and it made a really big difference at that point in my career.'

2. If you know your values, ambitions will follow

'What I'm seeing more of now is people realising they need to work out what ambition means to them and them alone. Your own definition will be different from your colleague, your friend, your partner, and it takes a bit of soul-searching to find – but when you do, it will change the way you work forever.

Start by noting down what your values are: these are the things that drive you in life, that make you feel happiest and most fulfilled. For example, mine are achievement, ideas, learning and variety – I know when I'm not getting enough of these four things in my life; I can feel stagnant. There have been moments where I've over-prioritised work and stopped doing something like playing sport because I've been so busy, but then I missed the achievement kick I got from playing netball matches at the weekend and ended up feeling worse in myself and worse at work. It was a bad decision for me, personally and professionally, but it reminded me that my ambition is only healthy when I'm tending to all four of my key values.

'Think about what is really important to you, and use that to redraw your ambitions. If autonomy is really important to you, maybe your ambition is to be self-employed one day. If helping others gives you energy, maybe your ambition is to dedicate a day a week to volunteering. If being around your family fills you up, maybe your ambition is to get to a place, financially, where you can spend most of your time with them. These ambitions are all just as valid and just as inspiring as "becoming the CEO" – and if they're conjured up with your own specific values in mind, working towards them is far more likely to make you happy.'

3. An ambition mentor will keep you on the right path

'Building a career community both inside and outside the organisation you work for can be so useful when you're feeling unmotivated or stuck. Think about people who share a similar ambition to you, or who have realised an ambition of yours and can share their experiences. Those are the people who will reignite the fire in you when you lose sight of what you're doing it all for. Don't be afraid to ask for help and prioritise creating connections – it does count as work. When it comes to mentors, people often worry about the give and gain, but humans are generally not so transactional; they want to share their wisdom. Build a network of people whom you admire and share a common ambition with, and you will flourish in their company.'

Journal prompts to help you hone your ambition

WHAT questions:

- What does a week well spent look like for me?
- What do the highs in my career so far have in common and what can I learn from my lows?
- What do I feel most proud of in my career and life so far and why?
- What would I like to be true in twelve months' time that isn't true today?

HOW questions:

- How do I define ambition?
- How can I narrow down my three main ambitions right now?
- How am I making progress towards my ambitions at the moment?

WHO questions:

- Who could be my ambition mentors?
- Who could I have a curious career conversation with?
- Who have I been inspired by in my career?

6. Boredom as a superpower

When was the last time you were really, truly bored? It's a feeling we remember well from childhood, contagious yawns spreading across the maths class and cries of 'I'm boooored' on rainy half-term days, but nowadays it seems like a distant emotion. There's always an email to send, a new podcast to get into, some life admin to tick off our to-do lists. Many of us can't even go to the bathroom without our phones in hand – even there, sitting idle has become impossible.

With 24/7 entertainment at our fingertips, it's easier than ever to avoid those quiet lulls. We listen to music while we walk, scroll through Instagram while we wait in a queue and lug a book or magazine around lest a five-minute window in our day open up that isn't spoken for. There's rarely a moment when our brains are not subject to some form of external stimulus. A 2014 study from the University of Virginia found that people 'typically didn't enjoy spending six to fifteen minutes in a room by themselves' and that 'many preferred to administer electric shocks to themselves instead of being left alone with their thoughts' – yes, really.

Even the world around us is built to protect us from nothingness: in a 2013 BBC report, it was found that buttons at many pedestrian crossings across the UK serve no purpose other than giving us something to fidget with, and in Mary Mann's 2017 book *Yawn:*

Adventures In Boredom, she writes that most 'close door' buttons in American lifts are simply there to help people pass the time.

Ennui evolution

So what is boredom, and why are we all so afraid of it? According to the *Oxford English Dictionary*, the word first appeared in Charles Dickens's grim Victorian saga *Bleak House*, published in 1853. (If you were forced to read all 1,088 pages of it at school, you might find that quite fitting.) Tolstoy described boredom in *Anna Karenina* as 'a desire for desires'. In fact, until quite recently, the best understanding we had of boredom came from literature – the world of science saw it as a trivial feeling.

Today, psychologists consider it to be one of the most understudied emotions. One of the area's leading experts is Dr John Eastwood, a psychology professor who runs a 'boredom lab' at York University in Canada and defines it as 'the uncomfortable feeling of wanting but being unable to engage in satisfying activity'. Eastwood says there are two key psychological mechanisms at play when we feel a bout of boredom coming on: the 'desire bind' – desperately wanting to do something but not wanting to do anything in particular – and the 'unoccupied mind' – the issue that whatever we're doing isn't exercising our cognitive capacity. The discomfort we feel when ennui strikes is written into our biological make-up. 'We're wired to want to be engaged with the world, exercise our abilities and realise our potential to stop us stagnating as a species,' Eastwood says. 'So we've evolved to find the state of being unoccupied quite aversive.'

But what if being bored isn't the negative emotion we think it is? Bruce Daisley, EMEA vice president at X, formerly known as Twitter, and author of *The Joy Of Work*, is a big advocate of the theory that an unoccupied mind is a fertile one. 'In our frantic lives and our hectic offices, many of us just don't have any space at all for those moments where our minds wander and we end up a million miles away,' he says. 'But there's so much evidence that our brains are at their most creative and prolific when they're in that state.'

The power of daydreaming

Daisley says that giving ourselves the chance to be bored is the key to sparking brilliant ideas. He uses the example of Aaron Sorkin, the Oscar-winning screenwriter and director behind *The Social Network* and *The West Wing*, who found that no matter how hard he racked his brains at his desk, inspiration was most likely to strike while he was unwinding in the shower. So, naturally, he had one installed in the corner of his office and proceeded to bathe eight times a day. Similarly, Bill Gates – arguably one of the world's greatest minds – knew the power of nothingness while he was head of Microsoft, carving out a biannual 'think week' when he would head to a hideaway to do nothing but ponder the big technological questions of the day.

One of the defining studies behind this link between a state of boredom and creativity was conducted by Dr Sandi Mann, psychology professor at the University of Central Lancashire and author of *The Science of Boredom*. She asked two groups to think up as many different uses for a pair of plastic cups as they could, but one group was given the mind-numbing task of copying from a phone book first. The study found that the boredom induced by the passive activity resulted in a 'daydreaming state' that helped them come up with more ideas afterwards. 'Doing nothing stimulates the creative juices, which means you can problem-solve and learn how to engage yourself,' says Mann. 'It's also stress-releasing because you come up with solutions to things that have been worrying you.'

When we look back to our childhoods, this relationship makes sense. As kids, stretches of free time lent themselves to imaginative play, when we created whole worlds in our heads and all fancied ourselves as crayon artistes. Today, parents have the dilemma of whether to leave a restless child to figure out how to entertain themselves, or opt for the quick fix of putting a device in front of them. But, just as adults reach impulsively for smartphones in quiet moments, resorting to the glossy lure of technology isn't always the healthiest thing to do. Experts compare it to eating junk food rather than putting in the effort to cook a nourishing meal.

'While you're watching yet another Netflix episode or mindlessly scrolling social media, you won't be bored in that moment, but the problem is that you've handed over control of your attention to an external force,' explains Eastwood. 'And it might not be satisfying in that deeper way because it doesn't flow from your own internal desires. Boredom is a signal emotion like pain or anger, warning us that something needs fixing, that what we're doing isn't good for us. So doing something to distract from that feeling, like getting drunk to numb pain or passively consuming something to alleviate boredom, isn't addressing the underlying problem.'

Feel the fear and do nothing anyway

It seems that in order to harness the power of doing nothing, we need to reset our relationship with boredom. Mann conducted another study – with fewer willing participants, she admits – in which people were asked to leave their phones behind and step into an empty, soundproof room. 'Obviously a lot of people ran screaming,' Mann says. 'But those who managed to stay said they found it pleasant after a while. They went through a pain barrier of boredom and then said it felt like respite, like having a hot bath.'

She has also worked with the Dull Men's Club, a group dedicated to 'celebrating the ordinary', who luxuriate in such mindless hobbies as composting and organising bookshelves. Many of these low-level thrill-seekers are also regular attendees of the annual Boring Conference in London, with tickets selling out to see impassioned talks on everything from the inner workings of inkjet printers to the similarities between different countries' national anthems.

This all might sound like a very British form of meditation, but even that has been packaged as a productivity-boosting endeavour to make it feel less indulgent. Admitting you sat and stared into space on your lunch seems less acceptable than, say, practising mindfulness or taking part in a sound bath. But experts say our thirst to understand ourselves and quieten our minds can actually be quenched by embracing tedium.

Eva Hoffman, a former editor at the *New York Times* and author of *How to Be Bored*, believes boredom is key to getting in touch with our true selves. 'In order for us to understand what we want or enjoy, we need to spend some time with ourselves,' she says. Eastwood agrees with this. 'The value of downtime is that it allows us to reclaim our agency. If we're constantly being stimulated from the outside, we can literally lose sight of who we are, what matters to us or why we're doing anything.'

Less work, more musing

Clearly, embracing boredom is an important life skill; it can help us work through worries and induce bursts of creative thought. But what happens when boredom strikes in the one place it's most frowned upon? According to a 2017 study by job site CV-Library, nearly forty-five per cent of UK employees are afflicted by boredom at work, and fifty-four per cent admit they've looked for a new job as a result – but in her early research, Mann discovered that boredom is also the second most repressed emotion in the workplace after anger.

This is no surprise. Few of us are comfortable with looking idle when we're being paid for our time, but the entrenched aversion to doing nothing from time to time could be making us unhappier and less efficient at work. 'A lot of the constant, frenetic activity in the workplace is to show that we're busy, because being busy is what makes you valuable,' says Hoffman. 'But if we're able to be a bit more thoughtful at work, then we can be more productive in the long run. A cultural shift is needed to allow room for that.'

Daisley, who has spent years examining the common pitfalls of workplace culture, bemoans our tendency to bounce between meetings and emails without any stretch of uninterrupted time to sit and generate something meaningful. 'Meetings are the enemy of good ideas,' he says. 'The average British person spends sixteen hours a week in meetings, then we get back to our desks and battle with never-ending inboxes. Our jobs sort of lose meaning. We have to remind ourselves what we're there to do and why.' And that means making space for empty time in your day; Daisley suggests turning off your notifications ('because there is always an email waiting to be

read, you don't need your phone to tell you that') and forcing yourself
to take a stroll or eat alone on your lunch break.

Give yourself permission

When it comes to free time, Hoffman says the first step is ridding
yourself of the guilt and judgement around being still. 'Understand
that hectic overactivity is not healthy and it doesn't make you better or
more productive,' she says. 'In quiet moments, slow down and let your
mind go in its own direction for a few minutes. It's not as structured as
meditation. Anyone can do it, anytime.'

In a world where we're all trying to slot more activities into our
already overstuffed diaries, it may be time to commit to doing a lot
more nothing. It's clear that we all deserve our own undivided
attention sometimes. So next time you're on a train, resist the itch to
scroll and try just watching the countryside roll past; rather than
automatically clicking that 'next episode' button, get to colour-coding
your bookshelves instead. Who knows, you might come up with your
next big idea or untangle that problem that's been bugging you all
week. Or you might just remember that spending time with yourself
isn't so terrifying, after all.

How to practise doing nothing

1. Be honest with yourself

If you find being still and unstimulated difficult, take a moment to think about why. Does it make you feel guilty? Are you worried it's not a productive use of time? Are you easily distracted? Whatever it is, note it down and consider whether it's a good enough reason to avoid a healthy moment alone with your thoughts.

2. Start small

Commit to five minutes of absolute nothingness every day. Put your phone on silent and shut off all distractions, then lie on the floor in a quiet room. Close your eyes if it'll help you relax, but don't feel this needs to be some mind-clearing meditation practice: the only goal here is to stay still and see what happens. Notice any impulses (to reach for your phone, or hop up and get a snack) then notice how quickly they can pass. After this layer of resistance comes the good stuff.

3. Be more cat

Try curling up or sitting in parts of your home you don't usually frequent – a random corner or a piece of furniture that rarely gets used. Cats are the masters of doing nothing, but you'll have noticed young children doing this too: the world is their playground and they let their imaginations run free. Mix up your vantage point and see if you don't feel a fresh spark of creativity.

7. Deep work or time-blocking? Find your productivity personality

Productivity: it's gone from buzzword to dirty word and back again. Most of us are productive in some capacity every day, whether that's finishing a project in your day job or cooking a meal on a Sunday night – to be productive just means to have something to show for your efforts. But in a society that values efficiency and output over all else, we can start to absorb the pressure to be productive in every waking moment, to fill our days with endless tasks and never leave a slot for nothingness or activities that don't necessarily result in a goal met or a tick off the to-do list. We can start to beat ourselves up for not being productive enough, although we're never quite sure what 'enough' would look like. This treadmill can be tricky to jump off, but it will have you heading straight for burnout.

On the other side of the coin, lots of us struggle to be productive in meaningful ways – particularly in our careers, where a set number of hours each week is dedicated to us getting something done, regardless of how we're feeling, how much sleep we've had or whether we're motivated. This is when we need to know how best to rev ourselves up and stay focused, when we start googling 'productivity hacks' or sit hoping for inspiration to land in our laps.

The pressure to do more and be more is everywhere, so if you're someone who's constantly writing checklists and looking ahead to the next task in your work and home life, you're absolutely not alone. But the essence of healthy productivity is really about working smarter, not harder – and not being hard on yourself in those natural moments when you just don't feel like doing anything. We are taught to fear those times when we don't feel motivated, to try to avoid them at all costs, but here's a truth the wellness adverts won't tell you: nothing can be done on motivation alone. It's far too fleeting a feeling, and far too much to ask of yourself. It's time to re-examine our relationship with the elusive spark that ignites our peak productive self.

 ## The motivation masterclass: When lightning doesn't strike
by Dr Julia Ravey

Dr Julia Ravey is a neuroscience PhD and the author of Braintenance, a scientific guide to working with our brains and their evolutionary quirks rather than against them. Here's what she's learned about how motivation manifests, and what to do when it doesn't.

Motivation is a survival mechanism
'Motivation is something most animals have, from humans to birds to worms, and it's a seeking behaviour that helps us pursue something that the brain thinks will be advantageous to us. Historically, human brains would have been motivated to seek things like sugar or high-energy food; a mate to secure the passing on of genes; companionship to up chances of survival. It's this ancient driving sensation that's essentially about keeping ourselves alive.'

We're wired for instant gratification

'Our brains are not motivated by action, they are motivated by the end result. Take waking up very early to catch a flight somewhere hot, versus waking up early to go to the gym before work. You know the former is going to be just as unpleasant in the moment, but the reward of the holiday is close enough that our brains are motivated to reach for it. Whereas working out for a more amorphous benefit at some point in the future is less motivating, it's not an immediate pay-off, and our brains are suckers for instant gratification. It's a similar story every January, when people set big goals that often require a lot of time and effort before they'll start to see any returns. Relying on motivation to keep chasing those goals is practically impossible, because we're just not wired that way – we're very present-biased.'

Don't rely on feeling motivated

'Motivation is one of those feelings it is important to act on when you do feel it, because it can put you in this elevated state. But it's even more important to act when it's not there, otherwise you're just confirming to your brain that you can only be productive when you feel motivated. Achieving any goal is more about consistency than motivation: carving out patterns that then become habits. Whether it's work, exercise or social plans, we always come to this crux decision point of "shall we do this now or shall we put it off?" and there is always a reason to put it off. In that moment, it's about cutting that thought off and deciding very quickly that you're still going to do it anyway.

'It's all about planning for your future self. I like to do it on a Sunday: plan my week out on a notepad and make sure it's as easy as possible for future me to follow that plan. Build up routines so that things become default, and the voice in your head that's resistant to "doing" will become quieter. Say you want to go on a walk every lunchtime as a non-negotiable – you know it makes you feel calmer and more focused in the afternoon. The first few times you do it, you will probably drag your feet and come up with reasons why you can't step away from your desk, but if you just keep going, eventually you will click into autopilot: when it's 1pm, you grab your coat and head out without overanalysing it.'

But do notice what energises you

'So now we know we shouldn't rely on motivation to power us through our days, but that's not to say we shouldn't try to spark it where we can. If there is a way you know you can generate some motivation – a certain person you follow on social media who inspires you or a song that always fires you up – you should absolutely draw on that in the moments where whatever you need to do next feels difficult. Find your own motivation recipe; mine includes a workout while listening to a fascinating podcast followed by a latte from a nice coffee shop, but everyone's will be different. Try and notice when you feel most productive and able to do meaningful work, then note down what might have contributed to that. You'll start to build up a list of motivation generators that you can keep in your back pocket and plant throughout your day to keep you going when you need to.'

The fact is, we're complex human beings, not machines or cogs on an assembly line. To keep ourselves focused and putting out work we're proud of requires a lighter touch, and it can be a very individual experience. Just because your colleague bounds into work talking about how they went to a HIIT class and had a breakfast meeting all before you'd even hit snooze, it doesn't mean that you could – or should – be doing the same thing. Everyone works differently, and figuring out what method is best for you is key to being productive in a healthy and satisfying way. If you know you're a person who focuses best in the quiet of night, don't try to force yourself to suddenly join the 5am club and tackle your to-do list first thing. Figuring out what kind of producer you are is the first step towards working smarter.

What's your productivity personality?

Choose a producer type that sounds most like you, then read on for the productivity method that can help you get more done.

The beaver

You're a grafter who puts in the hours, spending long stretches at your desk until the task is done. But things often take you longer than they should because you struggle to concentrate, easily distracted by pinging messages or the lure of a five-minute social media scroll that turns into half an hour. By the end of a working day, you tend to feel mentally drained, but may not have that much to show for it. If any of this sounds like you, read on to find out how the **deep work method** can help you stay in the zone.

The octopus

You're a multitasker, dipping into lots of different projects and spreading yourself thin. You may have lots of ideas and always feel the urge to get started on something new, but find you're less accomplished at seeing things through to completion. You're easily bored by working on one task for too long so you flit to another, but you never feel you're making real headway on anything. Read on to learn about the **time-blocking method** and how it can help you prioritise and organise your time.

The magpie

Your eyes are on the prize: a work-for-the-weekend type of person who is motivated by rewards, end results and a sense of achievement. You might also enjoy the satisfaction of ticking things off a list and need little pick-me-ups to keep you working. Read on to find out how the **Pomodoro Technique** can help make long stretches of work a little more appealing.

The Pomodoro Technique: best for 'magpies' and people who are easily distracted

Back in the 1980s, a university student called Francesco Cirillo started using a classic red tomato-shaped kitchen timer to help him organise his work. More than forty years later, Cirillo's time-management technique is now a huge TikTok trend, with social media influencers crediting it with helping them get all kinds of work done, from studying to cleaning their homes. 'The technique uses a timer to break down work into intervals, traditionally twenty-five minutes in length, and separated by short breaks,' explains Emma Jefferys, productivity coach at Action Woman. Although the practice is being touted as a saviour for people living with ADHD, the expert says, it can be used by 'anyone who wants to get stuff done and it is especially your friend if you recognise yourself as a productivity saboteur'.

What's the science behind the Pomodoro Method?

The Pomodoro Technique is basically like HIIT training, but for the brain. Jefferys says there are three main ways it helps to rewire our productivity.

It reduces boredom: Despite how counterproductive boredom is to getting stuff done, it's natural for us to lose attention or get distracted because our minds are geared to wander. The Pomodoro Technique is a great antidote for this because, she says, 'A short blast of focused work means we can fully engage in the task, and then when we [take a] break, our brains are naturally stimulated by the change of scene and activity – so that when we return, we are even more focused.'

It promises a reward: You don't need to be a psychology buff to know that reward is one of the greatest motivators. Jefferys says, 'As humans, we benefit both from intrinsic and extrinsic motivation.' Sometimes, knowing you have to do something isn't enough motivation; you need the added push of a reward at the finish line. She explains: 'By building regular breaks – the rewards – into our working pattern, we are more motivated to get our heads down and earn that break – especially as it is so tangible and in the near distance each time. It's a win–win, as we get the gratification of having made progress on the task and then the reward of the break itself.'

It stops multitasking: If you have a tendency to put off work by picking up other tasks, you'll know that multitasking can be more of a hindrance than a help when it comes to productivity. And that's because 'we are much more productive when we focus on a single task at hand', Jefferys says. She continues: 'The technique encourages us to enter a productivity zone for twenty-five minutes – phones off – and just focus on getting the thing in front of us done. Studies have proven that what you see as a harmless flit between activities actually costs you a whopping twenty-three minutes and fifteen seconds to refocus fully where you were! Monotasking is where it's at.'

Who can benefit from using the Pomodoro Technique?

According to Jefferys, there are three types of individuals who can expect improved focus and concentration from implementing the Pomodoro Technique.

People who procrastinate: The thought of committing to a hefty chunk of work can be daunting enough that we find any and every viable reason to put it off. If big tasks are your kryptonite, Jefferys insists this technique is for you, saying, 'It allows you just to commit to twenty-five minutes. Just set the timer and see what you can get done in that time. It chunks it down, takes the pressure off and reduces boredom – which is often why we procrastinate.'

People who are easily distracted: If you're losing chunks of time to mid-task social trawls, the Pomodoro Technique is just the thing for you, because it 'commits you to just a short blast of work with no interruptions or distractions'. As an incentive, she says, 'The Insta scroll can be your reward over a cuppa!'

People who find it hard to stay focused: A lot of people may be this way due to habit, but for some, a natural propensity to lose attention can be the sign of a neurodivergency such as ADHD. Jefferys says the impulse to focus on something else will still be there while you practise the Pomodoro Technique. But, she explains, 'Writing down the places your mind wanders to during the focus period allows you to stay on the task in hand – but [you will] also know you have captured where your brain wants to go next, for later sessions.'

How do you do the Pomodoro Technique?

Jefferys follows the creator Francesco Cirillo's original method to a T. She advises you break down the process into the following steps:

1. Choose a task you'd like to get done.
2. Set a timer for twenty-five minutes and set an intention to spend twenty-five minutes on this task without interrupting yourself.
3. Work on the task until the timer rings. If anything pops into your head and threatens to distract you, like an email you forgot to send, then just write it down and carry on.
4. When the timer rings, mark that down on a piece of paper and celebrate the fact you spent an entire Pomodoro productively.
5. Take a short break that is completely unrelated to the work you were doing. You can use this time to stretch, do a dance, make a drink or go for a short walk. Whatever it is, choose to do something relaxing and enjoyable.
6. Start all over again. Once you've celebrated four Pomodoros, take a thirty-minute break. This extended break will help to reset your brain, and make you feel ready for the next round.

Tips for making the Pomodoro Technique work for you

- Phones can be a source of distraction, so Jefferys advises using a kitchen timer or a stopwatch to time your intervals, as they're unlikely to distract you from the task at hand.
- If you're not keen on the idea of a buzzer or alarm going off to mark the end of a productive period, try creating a twenty-five-minute-long focus playlist to mark the time.
- The Pomodoro Technique is customisable, so play around with the focus periods and adjust break times accordingly. You'll know if you've made your intervals too long or short if 'you start losing focus and getting distracted, or you feel frustrated as you haven't got much done', respectively.

The deep work method: best for 'beavers' and people seeking creative flow

We all know that taking breaks from work is a healthy thing to do, both for productivity levels and mental health. Methods like the Pomodoro Technique are based around this exact principle, and many people have a lot of success using them. However, taking a break can disrupt the flow of your work, particularly if you're working on something creative or a task that requires a lot of concentration.

So how do you find the balance between taking breaks and getting stuff done? The deep work productivity method aims to answer this question. Created for specific tasks that require high levels of concentration, deep work encourages you to create a distraction-free zone and work for a set period of time without breaks. 'The brain can only concentrate properly for twenty to twenty-five minutes, but deep work allows you to work for longer if you can get into a flow,' explains Clare Evans, a time-management and productivity coach. This 'flow' Evans refers to is an intense state of concentration, and it's something you can learn by practising deep work regularly.

What kind of tasks should I do during deep work practice?

Deep work is designed for tasks that are going to take a longer period of time and might feel taxing on the brain, rather than quick easy tasks that you want to tick off a to-do list. 'Anything that requires a high level of concentration like strategic planning and thinking, working on difficult numbers, or doing something highly creative is perfect for deep work,' Evans says. This method works better for larger projects rather than individual tasks, particularly something you might be revisiting weekly or fortnightly.

How long should I practise deep work for?

The period of time you allocate to practising deep work is totally dependent on your personal needs. 'Some people might shut themselves off for a long period of time. For example, if they're writing a book, they might need one or two days per week,' Evans says.

Evans recommends setting one to two hours aside as a minimum for deep work so you can really get into your flow. You might want to start with a fairly small timeframe and build it up each week if you feel the method is helpful. Evans suggests practising deep work on a weekly or fortnightly basis. 'Schedule your deep work time into your calendar and block it out. Make it as non-negotiable as your commitments with other people because you need to take it seriously if you want it to be effective,' Evans adds.

How can I create a distraction-free zone to practise deep work?

Deep work allows you to get into a flow where it's easier to concentrate, but this will only work if you make it a priority to minimise distractions. 'Try and remove yourself from your normal office or working environment,' Evans says. She encourages booking yourself a meeting room in an office or leaving your house if you work from home to go to a café or working space where you won't be distracted by the doorbell or the people you live with.

'You should also switch off your phone and turn off email notifications. You could even set an out-of-office to say that you won't be available during this period of time,' Evans suggests. She stresses the importance of being clear with your boundaries so no one around you disturbs you. 'Think about what else distracts you when you're working. Make a note during your usual work week of any distractions that come up and find ways to minimise them during your deep work time,' she adds.

It's also important that you've eaten enough and done some form of exercise before entering a deep work flow, according to Evans, so you don't get hungry or feel fidgety while you're trying to work. 'Try your best to get a good night's sleep the night before, too, so you don't feel tired or sluggish,' Evans says.

What else can I do to make sure my deep work practice is effective?

As well as removing distractions, there are some other things you can do to improve your deep work practice. 'Set yourself realistic goals and make sure you know what you want to achieve during this time period,' Evans says. You might be able to do more than you expect during this time, if you really minimise distractions, but try to keep your goals achievable so you don't rush important tasks.

'Another thing I suggest is buddying up with someone and setting a similar goal so you can get into the flow together and hold each other accountable,' continues Evans. 'It also adds a slight element of competition which can be helpful.'

The time-blocking method: best for 'octopuses' and people who think visually

If lists, schedules and organisation help you focus your mind, this method may be the one for you. Time-blocking is the opposite of multitasking, which research from Stanford University found actually impairs cognitive control and makes people less productive. 'Time-blocking has changed my whole life,' says Lisa Johnson, a business coach and founder of That Strategy Co, who teaches the method to all her clients. Johnson started using the time-blocking technique when she started her own business four years ago and credits it with taking her from being £30,000 in debt to earning around £4 million a year because she was able to manage her time more effectively.

'Starting a business and being a mum to twin boys, means I have to really prioritise my time,' she says. 'Time-blocking helps me do that and means I only have to work thirty hours a month to make my money because I am so good at managing my time. You don't have to work hard, you just have to work smart.'

Here, Johnson explains everything you need to know about time-blocking and how to start doing it yourself.

Write down all your tasks

To start time-blocking your tasks, you must write down everything you need to do that week. 'And I mean *everything*,' says Johnson, 'Make sure your whole life is chunked, not just work, because then you'll get everything done.' This means things like ringing your mum, going to the gym or spending time with a friend should be in your time-block schedule too.

Make a spreadsheet schedule of your week ahead

The next step is to add these tasks to a spreadsheet and give each one a set amount of time in your week. 'On Monday, I'll plan that 7am to 8am is time just for me,' says Johnson. 'Then 8am to 9am is time with my kids. Then I'll divide the rest of my time into half-hour and hour blocks, each focusing on a specific task. When we make a list of everything we need to do, we always leave things at the end that never get done and keep getting put off from one week until the next. Whereas when you time-block, everything you need to do is already factored into your week.'

Remember, your phone doesn't control you

When it comes to getting things done, our phones can be a huge distraction. 'I used to look at my phone first thing every morning, and it meant I spent my morning getting distracted and not getting anything done,' Johnson says. She advises putting your phone on airplane mode when you're doing a specific task that you've blocked into your schedule so you can concentrate on it fully. 'Don't try to do a million things at once,' she says. 'When you see Facebook flash up, put your phone on airplane mode so you can't see it. If you want to scroll through social media mindlessly for an hour, that's fine, but time-block it into your day so you can do it for an hour without any guilt.'

Have an intention for everything you do

To make the most of what you've chunked into your day, Johnson suggests going into each task with a clear intention. 'If your intention is to play with the kids, then play with them and don't get distracted looking at your phone under the table,' says Johnson. 'If your intention is to make connections at a networking event, think about how you'll accomplish that before you do it.'

It's also important to factor in how you want to feel each week to be at your best. 'Do I need to be confident that week because I'm standing on the stage? Do I need to be calm that week because I've told myself it's about self-care? Always be intentional about your time,' says Johnson.

Don't prioritise quick wins

Prioritising tasks that we know we can get done quickly may feel good as you're ticking off your to-do list, but it can also mean we end up neglecting important things, according to Johnson. 'Sometimes we can spend two hours just getting rid of quick wins, like sorting through our inboxes, when actually it might not be the thing that we really need to do,' says Johnson. 'You may have played with your email for an hour and put off doing something really important. I time-block an hour into my day to deal with emails. That means when I'm doing my work, I'm not overwhelmed or stressing about other things because I've already time-blocked it into my day and so I'll do it.'

Time-block your time-blocking

As with all your tasks, you also need to factor in time to do your time-blocking for the week ahead. 'Every Sunday evening, I time-block in an hour to plan out my week so I'm not stressing about it on Monday,' says Johnson. 'I time-block out my whole week so I know exactly what's going to be happening and I write down my intention for what I want to happen that week.'

Don't worry, you can still be spontaneous

Just because you've got a schedule for the week doesn't mean you can't be spontaneous, Johnson explains. 'You can move things around and still have a structure,' she says. 'In the past, I've time-blocked my whole week and then decided to go on holiday at the last minute. It just means moving things around to accommodate that.'

Johnson also emphasises the importance of having blank chunks in your week. 'You can also time-block in time to do nothing . . . Life isn't a race, so give yourself actual free time. I have whole days where my time-blocking is "do nothing except whatever I fancy that day".

'Before I started time-blocking I used to prioritise work, and I think a lot of us do that over everything else,' says Johnson. 'But actually, if we want to be happy in life, we need to make sure we prioritise other things. With time-blocking, you won't feel guilty about it, because work time has already been built into your week.'

Beware toxic productivity

Toxic productivity is when your self-worth becomes tied up with how much you're doing with your time, and it can spiral into a really unhealthy aversion to rest and much-needed downtime. Signs that you could be slipping into toxic productivity include feeling guilty a lot for not doing enough in your job, or dedicating all your free time to 'useful' things like exercise or cooking rather than activities that are simply for the joy of it. If you find yourself struggling to sit still, or you're constantly thinking about your to-do list during the times you've set aside for resting, you're not alone. But it is something you need to tackle or it can quickly lead to overwhelm and burnout, because we humans are just not made to work incessantly. See Chapter 11 to get better acquainted with that equally important state: unproductivity.

A note on busywork

Busywork is the antithesis of true productivity: a task that doesn't have any real purpose or tangible outcome, but makes you (or your boss) feel like you're doing *something*. Often, in professional settings, the fear of being on the clock but not actually working pushes us into busywork: aimless filing, colour-coding, repeating something that's already been done. We assume it makes us look valuable, but in truth we're only wasting time.

On a personal level, it can be tempting to do something untaxing that gives us the glow of feeling productive but that in our heart of hearts we know isn't that useful. Often we do it because we're avoiding a much bigger and more difficult task. If you notice yourself resorting to busywork often, or find that you're being asked to do these kinds of tasks at work, it's worth a chat with your manager about how you can make a more purposeful contribution. It will show your willingness to make an impact, but it will also help you feel motivated throughout the day and more fulfilled at the end of it. It's never worth working just for the sake of working – life is just too short.

8. Why your emotions should run your career

You may not buy in to the idea that you should be happy at work, per se; maybe you just see it as a necessity, a means to an end. But most of us do want to spend our working hours doing something that at least doesn't make us *unhappy*, in an environment where we're comfortable, and yet a shocking number of us don't have that. The UK's largest ever study of work happiness was conducted by Indeed in 2022, looking at 1,800 organisations across twenty-five different sectors. It found that thirty-six per cent of all Britons were unhappy in their jobs. That's more than 24 million of us. (If you're interested, the unhappiest industry was real estate, followed closely by management and consulting. The happiest sector was education, in which workers scored highly on having a clear sense of purpose.)

Culturally, we are so used to divorcing our feelings from our work. Few of us ask 'Will I be happy in this job?' before we ask 'Will it pay the bills? Is it easily accessible? Do I have the skills?', and that is understandable, but it's a mistake to discount happiness, or at least contentment, altogether.

We tend to push down our emotions in the workplace, and around work in general, keeping calm and carrying on because we think this is just what it means to be an adult. Get through the day and take home the pay, no matter the impact it's having on our mental or physical wellbeing, not to mention our very life force.

But unhappiness is not a state we have to exist in indefinitely. It's an emotion we should sit up and pay attention to, because it's telling us that something isn't a good fit. It may be that your industry or role isn't allowing you to flourish or fully express your talent; it may be that the very way you are working, whether that's full-time or freelance, doesn't mesh with the life you want to lead; it may be simply that you've reached a natural end in your role and are craving a fresh start. Without tapping in to how your job is truly making you feel, you can't come to any of these critical conclusions.

Wherever you're at, learning how to tune in to the way you're really feeling when it comes to work will pay dividends over the span of your career, not only for your own health and success, but also for your relationships and leadership skills. Read on for the tools and techniques that will help you work with more feeling.

Seven ways to fix work unhappiness

Speaker and coach Samantha Clarke realised just how important happiness at work is after she noticed her clients continuously telling her how much of a negative effect their jobs were having on their lives. In response, she wrote *Love It or Leave It: How to be Happy at Work*, which explores how to love the job you're currently in or leave your job to start a new career that brings you real happiness.

Here, Clarke outlines seven common reasons why you might feel unhappy about work and offers tips for dealing with them to make your life more enjoyable.

1. Your job doesn't support your views around ambition and success

Most people will relate to one of two approaches to work, Clarke explains. The first is that you feel passionate about your career and you want your work to be a central part of your life. The second is that you view work as a way to make money to do the things you enjoy. Both are healthy approaches to work, Clarke says, explaining that the first approach can be extremely fulfilling and that the second outlook can 'fuel you to do other things in your life that you love'. The issue arises when your current job doesn't support your preferred approach.

How to fix it

Clarke advises figuring out which approach suits you and whether those needs are being met by your current job. Perhaps you're in a career that requires a lot of energy from you but you're not that invested in it and would prefer more free time to do things you enjoy. Or maybe there is another career path you would like to put more energy into. If one of these perspectives resonates with you, it might be time to look at a career switch. If not, and you feel like your work suits you, this probably isn't the reason you are feeling negatively about work.

2. You don't feel passionate about your role or industry

If you've started to lose interest in your role, this can affect how much you enjoy your job significantly, particularly if you're in a creative position that requires you to come up with new ideas on a regular basis. 'Sometimes when we're working at things that aren't our real strength, it exhausts us to the point of burnout,' Clarke says.

How to fix it

'You can craft your job to match your skills and your strengths and let go of the things that aren't working,' Clarke says. 'Identify which parts of your job aren't working and have a conversation about them with your manager,' she adds.

Clarke also explains that you don't have to feel passionate about every element of your job – it's OK for there to be some aspects you enjoy less. In fact, that can help you to make sure you have healthy work–life boundaries. 'Ask yourself where you find love outside of work,' says Clarke. 'If you're enjoying your job sixty to seventy per cent of the time and finding fulfilment in other areas of your life, you don't need to pour everything into one job.' If you're enjoying your job much less than that, however, and are feeling totally disengaged by work, it might be time to think about a career switch.

3. You're struggling with career progression

Perhaps you feel stuck in your role and you would like to move up within your company or industry. This can make you feel bored or restricted in your current role and this issue might also mean you're unhappy with your salary, which can have a negative impact on your overall impression of your job.

How to fix it

Often, the solution to this issue is applying for new roles at a higher level or speaking to your manager about a promotion. 'Identify your strengths, your skills, your passions and values,' says Clarke. 'You have to vocalise them and figure out how you can use them to move forwards to a role that allows you to achieve them.'

However, sometimes career progression can be stagnant. 'Maybe there's a hiring freeze at your company or maybe you feel unsure about whether you want to take on the responsibility that comes with a promotion,' Clarke says. If you're not being given a promotion at your current job, you might need to consider whether moving companies is a good option for you, she adds. If you're unsure whether a promotion is what you want, you may need to re-evaluate whether career progression is really what's making you feel negative about work.

4. You don't work well with your colleagues

The people you work with are a big part of how you experience your job. If you don't enjoy working with them, this can seriously affect the way you feel about your job and therefore your daily life.

How to fix it

'To deal with this, you need to understand why you're having conflict with certain types of people and what you might be able to do to cultivate more healthy relationships with them,' Clarke says. This could be down to a clash in personality types and working methods between you and your colleagues, which is something you can talk about and try to work through. Alternatively, it could be down to the way you work with other people – perhaps you might prefer working on your own, working for yourself or as a freelancer. Or you might need to work on your communication style. This is something you can do training on and reflect on in your own time.

Another issue is that one or more of your colleagues may be difficult to work with even after flagging these issues to them. If you have tried to communicate this to them and your managers and they continue to act in a way you find difficult to work with, the first step is to figure out if you can work less closely with them. If this isn't possible and you feel you've tried every other option, changing roles is the final option you could consider.

5. You're burned out

A common reason as to why people feel negatively about their work is that they're burned out, which can make you feel tired and exhausted all the time. 'I think we've got to question why we're choosing to over-function,' says Clarke. 'What lies might we be telling ourselves when we continue to over-deliver [even] when we're tired and burned out and it affects the rest of our lives?'

How to fix it

'Commit to switching off at a certain time,' advises Clarke. 'Make deliberate plans so you can finish work on time and try to be a bit smarter with the way you're working. Don't let something drag out for longer than it needs to.'

Put boundaries in place to make sure you're creating a good work–life balance. 'Be really honest with yourself about why you're not creating healthy boundaries in your life already. Are you scared? What are you scared of?' Clarke says, explaining that you might have to overcome certain fears to put boundaries in place, but ultimately it will be worth it.

It's also crucial that when you take time off, you feel like you're fully away from work. 'There needs to be a clear line,' Clarke says. 'You need to stop checking your emails for the time you're away and let people know you won't be checking them. You need to understand that if you don't switch off on your holiday, you can't expect to be refreshed when you go back to work. Be firm with yourself and enjoy the breadth of life.'

6. You feel unhappy about other areas of your life

'Sometimes work can be the place where we bury other problems from our lives,' Clarke says, explaining that negative feelings about work might be a sign you're feeling unsatisfied on a wider level.

How to fix it

Clarke cites four pillars of happiness within life: your work, the relationship you have with yourself, your relationships with other people and your home. Consider how you feel about each of these areas and try to understand if you're projecting dissatisfaction in a particular area on to your work. For example, have you lost touch with certain friends because you've been so busy with work? Have you stopped giving yourself enough time to wind down and relax because you're working so late? Try and change things up in your personal life to see if that makes a difference to how you feel about your work, Clarke suggests. 'Concentrating on these different areas might take your focus away from work.'

7. It's time to make a career switch

If you're dissatisfied with your career as a whole and feel drawn to a different path, the reason you're feeling negative about your job might be because it's time to make a career switch. 'I never advise people to stay in something that is still making them unhappy after they've tried to improve it,' Clarke says.

How to fix it

Making a career switch can be difficult but, ultimately, it is truly fulfilling. 'You have to make a plan to leave and consolidate what it is you want from your next leap – don't jump from one fire to another,'

Clarke advises. 'Think about what training you might need to do, how you're going to build a new network and give yourself a realistic timeframe to do it in.

'You also need to know how much money you have to give you a financial runway if you are making a change,' she continues. When you're figuring out what you want from your next step, Clarke recommends finding out what motivates you. 'Is it money? Respect? Creativity? Power? All of these things will drive your ambitions,' she says. 'Get critical with yourself and ask yourself when you have felt bliss over the last six months or year,' she adds, explaining that this will help you figure out which direction to go in. 'Ask people around you who will give you critical and honest advice about what they actually look to you for at work and what you're good at,' Clarke adds. 'Your purpose only comes through trial and experimentation – it's not something that will just land in your lap.'

Toxic workplaces: how to deal with a job that's getting you down

Author and journalist Cate Sevilla has been around the block when it comes to navigating the trials and tribulations of the modern workplace. Her time working at huge tech giants, like Microsoft and Google, as well as at smaller companies, like now-defunct women's publication The Pool, caused her to really question and interrogate our relationships with our jobs, and how we can improve them. In 2021, she released her debut book How to Work Without Losing Your Mind, a guide to shifting your relationship with your career, with the task of making sense of toxic workplaces at the centre.

Micromanaging: how to deal with an overbearing boss

Micromanagement in the workplace generally manifests itself through a colleague or a manager trying to control every element of your working output, generally resulting in anxiety and frustration on your part. To try and tackle this, Sevilla recommends working out exactly what processes are affecting your work and, potentially, your mental health.

'How does this micromanagement behaviour manifest itself on a day-to-day basis?' she says. 'Is this person looking over your shoulder? Are they messaging you all day asking for updates?' It's really important to identify the elements of micromanagement that are going on, and why they are affecting you.

Set a boundary

Once you've worked out the behaviour that is triggering for you, ask your colleague or boss to find an alternative means of communication they can use to 'manage' your work output. This sets a new boundary between you and their responsibility of ensuring you're doing your job.

'So you could say, for example, "Instead of you chasing for updates throughout the day, could we instead do a scheduled check-in?"' Sevilla suggests. She adds that it's a 'powerful' response to a toxic working environment to offer up an alternative working process, because it helps test out if things can change enough for you to thrive at this job.

Working hours: how to ensure you have some control over the time you spend at work

If you feel like you can't adhere to your start and finish times at work – and you feel guilty taking breaks – this is a sign of a toxic workplace and, Sevilla says, is often indicative of examples set from those working at the top of a company. 'If this is the example set by management, it can then be viewed as the way to be successful and get promoted in a job,' she says.

Set a boundary

Sevilla says that finding 'concrete ways' of requesting a boundary with your management and colleagues in this instance is key. For example, she encourages scheduling non-negotiable times in your day where people cannot book meetings, and declining any meetings that do conflict with these times.

'When discussing this with management and employees, explain that you need this time in the day to carry out various tasks,' she says. This may be met with negotiation, and she encourages being flexible and 'solution-focused' with setting out these new boundaries so that everyone gets what they need.

Personal life: how to make sure your private life is considered

Working hours aside, if you feel as if your working life is encroaching on your personal life and making a work–life balance impossible, this could be a symptom of a toxic workplace. To try and combat this, and safeguard your personal time, Sevilla says it's crucial to sit down and work out how you'd like your ideal work–life balance to look, and how work is stopping you from achieving that. Here are some questions to ask:

- Do you want to be 'logged off' completely at a certain time every day?
- Do you want to be off calls from a certain point in your working day?

- Do you want to be able to cook dinner at a certain time?
- What time do you need to mark as time for yourself?

After you've done this, you can start to set out what elements of your working day are encroaching on these goals for balance. Sevilla adds that any experiences of working remotely through the Covid-19 pandemic will help with this, as working from home for a large proportion of the year will have indicated to you what times of the day or rituals you need to preserve in order to establish boundaries between working and relaxing at home.

Set a boundary

Once you've got an idea of what changes to your routine you'd need to safeguard your personal life, it's time to schedule a conversation with a manager to see how plausible this is. Bear in mind that you may not get 100 per cent of what you're looking for, but be clear of what that is from the outset – is it a cut-off from responding to messages? Is it a zero-tolerance approach to work calls during your annual leave? Sevilla stresses the importance of consistency here, to ensure that this solution remains sustainable.

Creative space: how to make sure new ideas and thoughts are welcome

If you don't feel comfortable enough to suggest new ideas or break away from the norm, for fear of judgement, this could be a sign of a toxic workplace. 'At this point, it's almost like you're becoming too afraid to do your job, and this can be one of the worst parts of working in a toxic environment,' Sevilla says. She insists that an employee's 'psychological safety' to contribute without feeling anxious is imperative, not just to your progress but to your team's and your employer's.

Set a boundary

This time, Sevilla suggests setting new boundaries with your fellow employees – opening things up and asking them how they feel about the status quo. That way, if they're feeling the same, this could provide a way to broach this with your management as a way to make brainstorming ideas or meetings that much more effective.

You could also work on 'creating your own environment of psychological safety', Sevilla says, by leading by example. 'If you're running a meeting, make sure you're asking other people what they think. So you're displaying the behaviour that you want your management teams to be displaying. Make sure other people feel they're able to speak up in these meetings [encourage them to do so], volunteer your own ideas and make it clear to others that they can disagree.'

When navigating a toxic workplace, Sevilla says it's all about 'working out what's actionable and what isn't'. But if you find that your attempts at action don't work, and nothing changes, this may be the time to draw a line and think about changing jobs or teams. Drawing these initial boundaries, she says, is a way of proving you've done everything you could and have given your colleagues space to improve or change the situation. 'When tackling these issues, it's all about deciding what you need to change, then setting and enforcing those boundaries that allow for change to happen,' she says.

Should you turn your hobby into a job?

As children, we perpetually changed our minds about what we wanted to be when we grew up. But as the years go by, we are encouraged to set our sights on one specific career path. Lockdown changed that, however, as a poll of more than 4,000 people by Aviva found three out of five workers plan to learn new skills, gain qualifications or change their career altogether as a result of the pandemic.

One person who has eschewed the pressure to follow a strict career trajectory is Anni Domingo. The polymath has spent her life enjoying many different careers, including acting, teaching, social work and broadcasting (among many other areas of work). Now, in her seventies, she has entered another industry and published her first novel, *Breaking the Maafa Chain*.

'I'm a very inquisitive and curious person,' Domingo says. 'I was brought up to believe that you can do anything. You might not do it to the same level as someone else but you can certainly try. I believe that most people never reach their potential because of a lack of confidence or a failure to consider new things.' She adds that trying out so many new things in a professional capacity has helped her to build confidence and resilience. 'I've never felt bored in my career.'

Making a career switch and building a varied professional life is something you can do at any stage of life, no matter how established you are in your current career. Here, Domingo shares her advice for having a varied career path and exploring your passions professionally.

Don't set overly ambitious goals

Career-switching means finding new ways to think about success that don't necessarily fit with conventional ideas associated with career progression. The nature of trying out different things means that you might not necessarily progress in a job as quickly as you would if you were only focusing on one role or interest. Domingo's advice is to stop trying to be the best at everything and avoid comparing yourself to other people.

'If something interests you, see how far you can develop it,' she says. This might become a lifelong interest and career, or it might be something that works for you for a very short period.

Make the most of opportunities (and look out for them)

'The reasons I've changed careers throughout my life have often been circumstantial,' Domingo says. 'If an opportunity presents itself to me, I tend to follow it through.' She explains that you shouldn't only look for new opportunities when you're unhappy with your current job role. 'I'm always open to new things. Try not to block yourself or convince yourself that you can't do something. Be more open to new opportunities and don't worry about failing.'

Learn to compartmentalise

Having constantly pursued different careers simultaneously, Domingo has had to learn to balance different ideas and tasks at the same time. 'Compartmentalising is really important if you're going to have multiple careers,' she says. 'Change your mindset so you know that what you're working on now is the only thing you need to focus on. Everything else can wait.'

Compartmentalisation skills allow you to focus on the task at hand without worrying about the other things you may have to do, which can help you be more efficient. Part of effective compartmentalising also means carefully planning your time, so you know you have time to focus on everything in due course.

Have confidence in your transferable skills

Changing careers does not mean starting from scratch. There will be transferable skills you can take from any role to a new one, even if the jobs are totally unrelated. 'You often won't be conscious of how many skills you have because they come so easily to you now, so try to make a list of your transferable skills, even if they seem basic,' Domingo advises. 'Varied experiences are so valuable to employers so don't underestimate that.'

Consider unconventional employment options

Career-switching doesn't have to mean quitting your current job and starting a new one. In fact, Domingo says that despite having had so many different roles, she has never actually been employed by anyone. 'I've never wanted a permanent job because [not having one] gives me so much freedom,' she says. For Domingo, pursuing different careers simultaneously has not only given her flexibility, but also stability, alongside creative fulfilment. 'During the pandemic, theatres were closed so I couldn't direct, but I could still teach,' she says.

Know your worth

If you want to take on many different professional roles, Domingo says that it is crucial to know your worth. 'Don't do things for free or cheaply if you can avoid it,' she says. 'If this is your profession, you have to make that clear from the start and have confidence in your ability.'

Although you may lack experience specific to the role, your varied experiences will be of great value, so never undersell yourself. One of the main benefits of career-switching, according to Domingo, is that you always have new areas in which to find passion, which already puts you in a great position to excel in new roles.

The entrepreneurship masterclass:
How to turn your hobby into your job
by Polly Vadasz

Ever dreamed of turning your passion project into a legitimate full-time job? Polly Vadasz, the founder of the stationery brand Sighh Studio, has done just that. Here, she shares how to navigate work–life balance when you start to make money from doing the thing that makes you happy.

The highs and lows of the side hustle have long been part of our collective vocabulary – and it's actually a process that can take longer than you think. Polly Vadasz can vouch for this: she started creating phone cases for fun while she was at college. Almost a decade on, she runs her own successful business and employs multiple people.

Polly has some invaluable guidance for people looking to turn a hobby into a money-making venture, without squeezing the joy of it – from practical tips on how to start building a social media following for your brand, to advice on navigating a healthy work–life balance and maintain clear lines between work and play. Here's what she has to say.

Figure out if you're passionate enough about your hobby to make it your job

Doing something you enjoy for three hours or so a week is one thing, but doing it for forty hours per week is a whole new level of commitment. You have to decide whether you feel passionately enough about your hobby to commit yourself to it professionally. Polly struggled with this at first, but then someone asked her, 'Would you stay up all night drawing?' She realised that when she answered affirmatively, her passion was enough for her to turn her hobby into a business.

Polly also explains that she felt the most vocational towards drawing and designing, another important thing to consider. Sure, you might enjoy baking on the weekends – but does baking for strangers and planning the logistics of that appeal to you too, for example?

'The second I start washing dishes, my brain goes to [illustrating] – that's what I find fun,' Polly says. Polly explains that she doesn't see herself as an artist, but rather as a designer who designs things for a purpose. This purpose and intention that came with her designs is what helped clarify Polly's ability to monetise her hobby. 'Don't feel pressured into selling if you don't want to, if it takes away from the creativity,' she says. 'But for me, I want to earn money in a way that I love and I love creating things.'

Be prepared to take on multiple roles

'Think about how many hats you wear as a small business owner,' says Polly. 'It's everything. It's admin, accounting, marketing, photography, design, merchandising.' Part of your job will actually be doing the hobby that you enjoy – in Polly's case, designing collections – but running a small business also requires you to take on a lot of roles that might appeal to you less, so it's crucial to decide whether those elements are a) something you can handle and are able to do, and b) something you are willing to do in order to make your hobby into your career.

Realise that your hobby won't be something you do for fun anymore

Although it's amazing to do what you love, it can be difficult to strike a good work–life balance when your hobby becomes your career. Polly suggests setting boundaries so you're not working on your passion outside of set hours, and also finding other hobbies that you can do in that time. 'I started pottery, painting, cooking,' she says.

Put yourself into your product – that will be its unique selling point

'I can't design things that I don't like,' Polly says. 'If I don't like a product, I won't market it properly.' Polly's genuine passion for her products is what has made Sighh so successful, and this has also allowed her to continue to find creativity and freedom in her job. 'Think about what you actually want to see in the world,' is Polly's advice for creating products that you like but that will also appeal to other people.

Don't overthink working with suppliers as a small business

If you are creating a product that requires you to work with suppliers, like designing clothing, candles or, as in Polly's case, stationery, you may feel intimidated by having to buy the materials you need in bulk. But Polly explains that the process is simpler than you might think. 'Finding suppliers is literally typing "custom space printing" or "custom notebook printing" into Google and then looking at all the websites.'

'Think about what you want to make,' is Polly's advice when it comes to finding the right supplier. 'Do you want a really shiny sticker? Do you want a notebook with lined pages? Do you want to design your own pages?' These kinds of details will help you narrow down suppliers. Polly also advises considering which places offer the most affordable minimum orders.

In terms of quality, Polly recommends investing in the best-quality materials you can afford, but adds that it's totally fine to upgrade your products' quality as your business grows. 'I always try and get a sample before I place an order,' she says, explaining that lots can go wrong with physical products, so it's good to check that you actually like what you're making before ordering it in bulk.

Polly started Sighh using a pre-order model, which she recommends, as it meant there was no upfront fee and she could also ensure she was ordering the correct amount of product from suppliers. She also stresses that your upfront costs don't have to be high straight away in order to turn over a high profit, '[The first] upfront costs for my business were about £70 and within a year, I took £70,000.'

Make your marketing personal

Polly has two Instagram accounts: a personal page where she documents her daily life and an account for Sighh that is limited, for the most part, to content about the business. She explains that her approach to marketing is very personal: 'I have an idea about something I want to see and then I show everyone how excited I am about it.'

'I've always been the main influencer for my shop,' Polly says. 'This is where personal, small businesses differ from large businesses.' Big businesses want you to buy in to the lifestyle of their brand, Polly explains, but with small businesses, the consumer often buys into the person behind it. 'I live my brand because my products are so me, and that works,' she says.

Build a community of people on social media who love your brand

'Encourage customers to take photos of their products and post them,' says Polly, explaining that you can do this by re-posting their photos on your business's social media page and including a compliment slip with their order which encourages them to take a photo of their order and tag the brand on social media. 'I would do giveaways for the best customer photo of the week,' Polly says. 'Just think about giveaways as investing – that's your investment. Giving away free products doesn't cost very much for the business.'

Practise caution when it comes to making your hobby your full-time job

'A really normal path is to have a full-time job or a part-time job and then do this on the side,' Polly explains. 'And then slowly, you need to take the risk of winding down those hours and focusing on your small business.

'But you shouldn't take a risk unless you see it growing,' she continues, adding that, in order for you to leave your job or reduce your hours, you should get to a point where you think you can no longer manage both and then consider what your priorities are and then, if you feel passionately enough about your business, take a risk on it.

Although Sighh is Polly's full-time job now, she spent a long time working part-time and also had the safety net of university early on in her small business journey. Taking small risks has got her where she is now, but so has carefully saving and ensuring she has safety nets to fall back on. Both are equally important for establishing your small business.

Why being more emotional at work could transform your career
by Natalie Boudou

With more than thirty years of experience in the corporate world, Natalie Boudou is the founder and CEO of workplace culture specialists Humanforce and the author of a book of the same name. She's passionate about sharing the ways in which we can reframe and reintegrate emotions into our working lives.

'For a long time, emotions have not been portrayed as a good thing in the world of work. In the past, logic or reason has always seemed to be the most important thing, whereas emotions have often been seen as a weakness, and not appropriate in a professional setting. And these beliefs have solidified over decades and decades of working culture, so lots of us can feel a bit awkward about expressing our feelings at work.

'When we work within a culture where it doesn't feel safe to emote, which is the case for a lot of people today, then we're not necessarily going to open up very much because we worry we won't be respected or taken seriously. We think we might be judged for it, it might impact our careers.

'There is also an internal bias that some of us hold about what is acceptable at work. A lot of people think it's OK to show happiness and be positive, but the opposite is a no-no – you can't be sad at work. Nor should you show fear, or frustration, or any other negative feeling, no matter how natural it is. We are taught, and we teach ourselves, to push those feelings down and perform in our daily lives.'

Work selves vs real selves

'The problem with being in a place for such a large chunk of your life where you're not able to express the full range of your emotions means you end up masking. This is something that people of colour in predominantly white workplaces, or LGBTQ+ people in predominantly straight spaces, are kind of forced to do all the time, in that we don't feel able to bring our whole selves to work. And when you're hiding your sadness, your anger, your fear, your frustration for eight hours a day, that's what you're doing – you're masking. That can lead to pretty poor mental health, all that hiding and not being able to acknowledge or express what's going on inside you. It also means you're not able to easily access your feelings and express when something at work isn't working for you or it's making you uncomfortable, which isn't healthy or conducive to a happy work life.

'The thing is, there are so many areas of work where we need to bring our emotions. When we're handling a difficult conversation, or giving constructive feedback, or talking to someone who's very stressed. When we're trying to innovate and create a new product, make a decision – in all of these common scenarios, bringing emotions into the equation can be very powerful, because our emotions are signals, they guide us. If we go into the workplace like robots, we're not doing ourselves justice and we're not bringing our full potential to the table.'

Leading with feeling

'It's crucial to building good professional relationships too. If somebody doesn't show any emotion, you don't trust that person, you struggle to understand where they're coming from. For leaders, especially, to build a bond and build trust within their teams, you need to be able to be vulnerable sometimes and honest about how you feel. That's what creates connection.

'Unfortunately, the idea that a good leader is all about command and control, focusing on results and delivery, is still there. But it is slowly shifting and there are some workplaces which are really trying now to bring in leaders who are human-centric, who are focused on their people and who understand that by investing in their people, they're going to get the performance they need.

'Somebody once asked me to compare Richard Branson, founder of the Virgin Group, and Elon Musk, who runs Tesla, SpaceX and X. I said, well, they are both business geniuses, but Elon Musk doesn't connect and Richard Branson does. He uses his charisma and also his emotions to get people to follow him and like him. I think he's a good example of somebody who has a lot of emotional intelligence and has used that to great effect at work.'

All emotions welcome

'The energy-draining emotions, which I prefer to call them rather than the "negative" emotions, are very important at work. They have a message for us. For example, if we feel angry, it's because we feel something or someone hasn't been respected, or that a boundary has been crossed, and sometimes that anger can be very useful. It's the same emotion that urges people to go out and march in the streets and protest against injustice, right? It makes them seek repair and positive change.

'Also, when a colleague leaves or we lose a project or a promotion, or there's a change within teams, that can be sad. And it's only when we're able to actually feel and express that sadness that we can let go of what we just lost, otherwise we remain in a sort of limbo state of not being able to process it or talk it through. There's nothing wrong with accepting and acknowledging how we feel, but toxic positivity can crop up a lot in workplaces – it's often, "Chin up, let's show we're happy and excited about everything even when we're not." But these energy-draining emotions are really important because they are usually telling us to do something that will improve our working lives; they help us identify issues or problems.'

Working more authentically

'For someone who feels they aren't able to express themselves emotionally at work, the first thing I'd suggest is figuring out exactly what you find difficult. Is it that you know how you feel but you don't know how to express it in a professional setting? Or is it that you struggle to identify how you feel full stop?

'The biggest tip I would give and the first tool I use to move towards emotion is to develop a sort of mindfulness within the working day. Can you see patterns in how you feel and notice what the cues are? It's good to have moments in the day where you're disconnecting for a moment and you're just being present with yourself and checking in on how your mind and body feel, because when we're running around and constantly doing, thinking about the past or the future, we're not able to observe how we're feeling. Those quiet moments allow you to catch your emotions and get out of that robotic mode, and in turn you can ask yourself why you might be feeling them and what that's telling you.'

Journal prompts to help you
unlock your emotions at work

- How does my body feel right now? What do I notice?
- Which emotions have I felt most strongly today?
- What may have triggered those emotions?
- What could they be telling me about the way I'm working?
- Which person or group could I express these feelings to?
- What would I like to feel more of, in relation to my work?
- What would I like to feel less of?

WELLBEING

9. Why mindfulness is *not* meditation

With roots in Buddhism and ancient meditation techniques, mindfulness is something humans have been doing for centuries. In fact, it's a natural state of being for us, but as our lives have become busier, noisier and far less punctuated by moments of quiet presence and awareness, the importance of being intentionally mindful has grown.

At its heart, mindfulness is just about noticing. Noticing what is happening both inside you – within your body and your mind – as well as around you. As simple as that sounds, most of us can go for hours if not days on a kind of autopilot, ruminating on the past, thinking about what we need to do in the future, and not really noticing on a conscious level how we're feeling, the thought patterns we keep falling into, or even the way the leaves on the trees are brushing against our office window.

The way we live is to blame for this sort of sleepwalking. Researchers at the University of California San Diego have found that in the modern world, the human brain is inundated with 34GB of information every day, enough to overload a laptop within a week. We barely have the time to parse or process even a small fraction of this information, leaving us with feelings of anxiety and overwhelm that we're not sure what to do with or how to mitigate. Mindfulness is a chance to be still, designated time that allows our brains to sift through that information and notice the effect it might be having on us. It's one of the simplest and most effective tools in tackling feelings of overwhelm, and one of the best ways to really get to know ourselves and our own needs better.

It's also a practice that, ironically, lots of us might feel we don't have time for, and that we may have tried once or twice and then feel we've 'failed' at because we struggled to quiet our busy minds. But mindfulness is not about trying to clear your mind or push down your thoughts. In fact, it's quite the opposite. It's time to think differently about a daily tool that may be the most transformative thing you can do for your wellbeing. The best part? You need nothing but your brain.

 ## The mindfulness masterclass:
How to see the world in technicolour
by Karen Glass

Karen Glass is a physiotherapist and mindfulness teacher who has run programmes for stressed-out NHS staff. She came to the powerful practice as a student, and though she was sceptical at first, she soon discovered how life-changing it could be.

What is mindfulness?
'Often, mindfulness is confused for an escapist technique or a shortcut to relaxation, but that's not really the aim. Mindfulness is really about getting to know yourself. It's taking a look around inside yourself with a gentle and non-judgemental attitude, getting to know the internal landscape of your own thinking and emotions as well as your body's physical sensations. And it's a

natural state for us – we are all in a state of mindful awareness from time to time – so it's not something you need to try hard at or become "good" at. It's a deeply intuitive way of being. You may just need to learn how to access it and practise it to feel the full benefits. It is dose dependent, just like medication or exercise.

'Mindfulness is about insight, understanding the roots of your own suffering, and suffering less so you can thrive more – that's the absolute crux of it. The distinction we make in the mindfulness community is between pain and suffering. Because yes, life is full of emotional and physical pain – that's just part of being human and we will all experience some of it. But suffering is the more optional part; we can do something about how we respond and react to things that happen to us in life, and that influences how much we suffer. That might sound heavy, but it's also about being joyful. Learning to suck the juice out of each day, in each moment, and being able to find amazingly beautiful things in the ordinary and everyday.'

Why should I start practising mindfulness?

'Jon Kabat-Zinn, who is known as the grandfather of secular mindfulness, said building a mindful practice was like weaving an emotional parachute: when it's time to jump out of a plane and do something hard or scary, you've got that parachute to ease you down gently.

'It enhances my own life day to day by helping me feel more content and deal with stress. There are two elements: one is the physical part, the awareness of my body. I've become really sensitive to picking up when my body is telling me it's not happy or I'm pushing myself beyond a limit, whereas before I might've been on the verge of burnout or overwhelm and hardly noticed. That allows you to take some wise action before things get too much, because your body and your breath can really alert you when something isn't right. So it helps you become more in tune with yourself, physically.

'It also helps you really understand and prioritise what matters to you, because you become more aware of how certain behaviours, people and situations make you feel. For example, you might notice that, actually, it feels really good to connect with a friend, even though it might have felt like a big effort to go and meet them before the fact. Or you might notice that it made you feel great to walk for half an hour in the sunshine. Mindfulness helps reinforce those behaviours and enhances the joy of them.'

Is mindfulness right for everyone?

'Mindfulness is so powerful and goes so deep that there also has to be a little bit of caution around it. Say somebody has experienced trauma in their life; it could be childhood trauma, an ongoing traumatic situation such as domestic abuse, or a one-off incident like a road traffic accident. In those situations, I'd always recommend you practise mindfulness with a teacher so you're supported with whatever might come up for you. Another caveat is if somebody has an existing mental health problem – for example, schizophrenia or psychosis – then I would say avoid dabbling in mindfulness on your own and get the guidance of a mental health practitioner.

'If you are recently bereaved, I'd suggest that you don't practise mindfulness for around six months or so, because there are some times in life where it might feel a bit too much to bring that level of awareness and focus to your mind, when actually having the defence mechanism of being busy and distracting yourself from what's going on internally might be the healthiest thing for you. So there is a bit of safety netting that is worth bearing in mind around this very powerful skill.'

Where do I start?
'The key element of mindfulness is what we call an "insight practice". Basically, the intention is to train your awareness and attention, but you'll also be revealing insights to yourself as you do this.

'Go somewhere quiet and close your eyes, then pay attention to the sensations of your breath as it enters and leaves your body. Naturally, you'll be able to do that for a few seconds and then your attention will drift away because you'll quickly get bored. Your mind will probably go back to a regular thought pattern that you're having in that moment, say something big is going on in your life like you're buying a new home or you're changing jobs or you're waiting for a medical result. That is likely where your mind will drift, so you notice that and then bring it back intentionally to focus on your breath. It will drift again, and you'll notice it and bring it back. It's a gentle steering and training of your attention, and straight away it will highlight where your mind is wandering and what is taking up the most brain space for you in that moment.

'Notice what that internal chatter is. Are there any themes you can pick out? For example, a very common one is self-criticism: I'm not good enough, I'm not rich enough, I'm not beautiful enough, I'm not fit enough. It's so common in our society to not feel "enough", and so maybe that's where your mind is going most often. Perhaps it's a habitual worry that your mind keeps snagging on: ruminating on the past, worrying about the future. Whatever it is, try to name it and just notice it.

'A mindful person is someone who can see themselves from a bit of a distance; it's a concept called metacognition, which just means there's a part of our brain that is observing the rest of us. It sounds very technical, but it's simply being able to sit there and be aware, and the more we practise it, the more it will become a second nature thing we can do in our day-to-day lives.

'I like to call it the "hot cross bun of awareness": there's the thought, the emotion, the physical sensation and the impulse. A thought might cross your mind, like "I didn't like the way my colleague spoke to me at work today"; the emotion might be anger; the physical sensation is a tightening in your chest; and then the impulse comes to send a flame email or start ranting about it to a friend. Even just noticing those different elements helps expand your understanding of how your mind works and how thoughts and emotions are just small pieces of the puzzle, not necessarily the things you should act on. You can view yourself with a bit more curiosity and be less caught up in the impulse or the habit, which gives you more of a chance to respond in a considered way that is best for you. I like to think of it as "slowing down the video".'

How to be more mindful in your everyday life

As well as meditation and the insight practice described above, there are ways to extend the benefits of being more mindful into the rest of your day, too. Try these tips when you feel busy, overwhelmed or disconnected.

In the shower

It's something many of us do every morning, so embedded in our routines that we practically sleepwalk through it. But this act of self-care is a perfect moment to check in with yourself and be present. Feel the sensation of the water on your skin, the lather of your shampoo, the smell of your soap. Notice the temperature in the bathroom as it changes, listen to the sound of the taps. You're guaranteed to feel more grounded and refreshed when you step out.

On a walk

This is something that we rarely do, so it might feel odd at first, but when you're walking somewhere, try to give that sole act your full attention. Resist the urge to reach for your phone, or put in headphones, or mentally run through what you've got to do when you reach your destination. Just focus on the motion of your body, your feet hitting the ground, the sights and sounds and smells around you. You'll notice so much more, and it'll make you feel more connected to the world and yourself. You might even see something beautiful or inspiring, or make eye contact and exchange a smile with someone you'd otherwise have missed.

At mealtimes

We get it, the urge to watch something on Netflix while you tuck into your dinner or open a book over lunch is real, but eating mindfully has benefits that go way beyond just your mind. Our senses of sight, taste, smell and even touch are all closely linked when it comes to what we eat, and by engaging them all we get more joy and even greater health benefits out of our food. Mindfully chewing, noticing how much we're putting into our mouths with each bite, and recognising when we're beginning to feel full up reduces bloating and aids digestion.

In conversation

Truly noticing the person you're with can have a profound effect on your sense of connection with them – people can tell when they're really being heard. Don't get distracted by devices, and don't start formulating the next thing you want to say rather than tuning in to what they are saying; be an active listener. Be aware of their expressions, their tone of voice and the way they're using their body – most experts suggest that around ninety per cent of human communication is non-verbal.

Mindful drawing masterclass
by Fiona Meakin

Mindful drawing has emerged as an alternative to classic meditation in recent years, with adult colouring books and life-drawing classes gaining popularity. Even if you think you're bad at drawing, it might be something you find relaxing now, particularly as the whole point of mindful drawing is to remove the pressure that often comes with creating art.

'You don't have to consider yourself to be a good artist to draw mindfully,' says Fiona Meakin, an artist based in Manchester who runs mindful drawing classes for children and adults. 'It helps you get into a mindful flow, similar to the flow people can get into when they're meditating, so it can be a really helpful tool to help you relax and look after your mental health.'

Mindful drawing not only helps you to take some time for yourself, it's also a creative act. 'It helps you reclaim your childlike self. Kids love to draw and it's one of the first things they can do when they pick up a pen, so try to channel that,' Meakin says. Mindful drawing is not totally dissimilar to conventional drawing, but there are certain things you can prioritise and focus on to make it a mindful experience. Here, Meakin shares her advice on how to get started with it.

Become aware of your body

Meakin encourages her students to think about their posture and become aware of their different body parts before beginning their mindful drawing practice. 'Just like in yoga, it's beneficial to think about your posture and your breathing,' Meakin says. To start, make sure your feet are planted firmly on the ground and try to relax your shoulders. You could even do a body scan (see page 247), tensing and relaxing different parts of your body and paying attention to the sensations in each one, to make sure you feel relaxed. 'It's also a good idea to do some breathing practices before beginning to try and let go of any tension you might be holding,' Meakin suggests.

Create a relaxing environment

One of the best things about mindful drawing is that it's really accessible and requires very little equipment. In fact, according to Meakin, all you really need is a piece of paper and a pencil. If it's something you enjoy, you could also invest in a sketchbook and some different coloured pens or pencils – because who doesn't get a dopamine hit from a new stash of stationery?

Meakin stresses the importance of creating a relaxing environment for mindful drawing. This doesn't mean you need a dedicated room, per se; it's about preparing and setting up a space that feels intentional, rather than whipping out your pad in front of the telly. 'Put on some music you like and clear the space. You can also light a candle or bring anything else into the room that might relax you,' Meakin suggests.

Start by scribbling

'I always encourage people to start their mindful drawing sessions by scribbling, as this can let go of a lot of tension,' Meakin says. Take five to ten minutes to scribble whatever you'd like, trying not to think about the outcome. This will stop you from associating drawing with creating a perfect artwork. 'A blank page often feels scary, so scribbling will help you get over this fear.'

Let your feelings come out through your pencil. 'If you feel stressed or angry, place that energy into your scribbles. Or if you feel sad or confused, your scribbling might be more of a process of trying to figure out your emotions,' Meakin says. Let your hand guide you and be curious about the end result.

Draw intuitively

The subject of your mindful drawing practice is totally down to you and the way you're feeling. 'To start, ask yourself how you want to feel by the end of your session and create an affirmation to reflect that,' Meakin says. You can either write your affirmation down on your paper or think about it while drawing.

From there, work intuitively by drawing freehand and perhaps coming up with an abstract design. However, if you're a beginner, Meakin says that this might be difficult or intimidating at first, so it can be a good idea to go in with an idea of what you might like to draw. 'Something simple like flowers is always good,' Meakin says, adding that you can even copy a photo or another drawing if that helps to boost your confidence.

'Don't worry about getting it perfect. Focus on the simple shapes you're trying to create, one at a time – remember that this is just for you.' She recommends spending no more than an hour on your mindful drawing practice, as spending any longer might encourage perfectionist habits. 'The great thing about mindful drawing is that it works even if you only have five or ten minutes.'

Don't erase your work

The most important thing about mindful drawing is that you avoid getting upset or annoyed about how your drawing looks. 'If you do start to get stressed about how it looks, leave that drawing there and start a new one or take a break,' Meakin says. Getting frustrated can be a natural reaction in a world where we're told only to do things in order to improve at them, or to produce something worthy in the end, but with mindful drawing it's the act itself that's the point.

'Try not to rip pages out or rub your drawings out,' Meakin says. 'Don't overthink your drawings and don't worry if you don't like how they look.' She says that accepting whatever the outcome of your session looks like can help you reframe how you deal with stress and uncertainty in your regular life, and find positives in every process. She also suggests that coming back to your drawings at a later date, especially the ones you didn't initially like, can be therapeutic. You'll be surprised at how often they're better than you remembered.

Journal prompts for mindfulness

Sharpen your focus and turn your attention inward with these journaling prompts – you may be surprised at what comes up.

- *What is one thing in my eyeline that brings me joy?*
- *What three emotions are strongest in me right now?*
- *What am I procrastinating on?*
- *What has made me feel good most recently?*
- *What thought do I keep having or going back to?*
- *How does my body feel right now?*

10. Good stress, bad stress

It can often feel like stress is part and parcel of modern life. Recent studies have described the UK as a 'stressed nation', with seventy-four per cent of adults feeling so stressed at some point over the last year that they've felt overwhelmed or unable to cope. Collectively, we're in a precarious position.

Stress is a physiological response in the body that happens when we feel threatened or under pressure. 'We've all heard of fight or flight,' says Claire Davis, a stress management consultant and founder of Midlife Mentors. 'We've inherited this from our ancestors, so it's in our DNA to be wary of danger. But while this was useful for our ancestors, who operated in pure survival mode, now we're responding to stressful events, like an urgent email, in the same physiological way, and we've normalised it. So we're sitting in that constant hum of stress.'

There are some newer schools of thoughts that are stripping the concept of stress right back to its roots as a survivalist signal, and trying to reframe what seems to be an inevitable part of life so we can actually use it to our advantage. Is there such a thing as good stress? Some would answer 'yes'; that in small doses it can inspire self-knowledge, great acts of problem-solving and creativity.

But before we get to those new ideas, let's tackle the age-old problem: an unhealthy kind of stress that has consumed us all at some point or another. Here are two tried-and-tested methods for managing stress, straight from the mouths of leading experts.

Practical ways to manage overwhelm: The ABC model

Being able to control our response to events we find stressful can help us cope and deal with stress, which is where a useful method called the ABC model comes in. The ABC model was created by an American psychologist called Dr Albert Ellis and then adapted by Dr Martin Seligman. It works by helping us to understand what situations trigger our stress response, why it happens and what it causes us to do.

'The key to the ABC model is recognition,' says Dr Audrey Tang, a psychologist, mental health and wellness expert and author of books on mindfulness and resilience. 'The model can help you get to the root of what's making you stressed and help create practical ways to overcome it.' Here, Claire and Dr Tang explain what the ABC model is and how you can use it in day-to-day life to help you deal with stress more easily.

What is the ABC model?
The ABC model is derived from cognitive behavioural therapy (CBT) and helps to explore why we react to certain situations in certain ways. The 'A' stands for 'adversity' or, in Seligman's model, 'activating event'. 'This is the trigger that sets off your stress response or your heightened emotion,' says Dr Tang. 'I prefer to use Seligman's

wording because an activating event could be positive or negative; either way, it's an event or situation that's going to send us into a heightened state of emotion where we act irrationally.'

'B' stands for 'beliefs'. 'When the activating event happens, it will trigger a set of beliefs in us,' says Dr Tang. 'These are automatic thoughts you start thinking when that event occurs.'

Lastly, 'C' stands for the 'consequences' that the activating event and your belief system around it create. To explain this, Claire uses the example of being stressed about giving a work presentation. 'The activating event is your boss emailing you and telling you to give a presentation,' says Claire. 'This might lead to beliefs like "I'm not good enough", "The last time I did that, I failed", or "No one will listen to me". The consequence of this is that you feel stressed and worried, you have an accelerated heart rate and you can't sleep.'

Reflecting on the ABC model

Usually, our brains go through the reactions in the ABC model so quickly that we don't know we're doing it. However, knowing how the model works means we can use it to reflect on stressful situations and analyse why they've made us feel this way. Once you have a better understanding of what causes you stress, you can equip yourself to deal with it better.

'When we're in a point of crisis, we won't necessarily be able to go through A, B and C,' says Dr Tang. 'But, afterwards, when we're away from that point of crisis, it can help to sit down to reflect, process and deal with it.' You can do this simply by thinking through the ABC model when you have some quiet time to yourself, or by writing it down. 'Journaling can be really transformational and can get us out of our heads,' says Dr Tang.

Analysing the activating event

Understanding what has triggered our stress or heightened emotion can help us plan around it, avoid it or take steps to minimise it. 'When we're writing down activating events in a journal, it can help us to establish the root cause – it may not always be what we initially think,' says Dr Tang. 'You might think, "My sister really annoys me every time I see her", when really it's something else your sister embodies that makes you feel stressed.'

'It's always useful to think about whether we can minimise the trigger or activating event,' says Claire. 'For example, if there's a certain friend who really winds you up, could you put more boundaries down?' However, Claire explains, 'We can't minimise all events, in which case you have to think about how you respond to it instead.'

Reflecting on our beliefs and changing the consequences

Reframing our beliefs about an event can help us change how we react to it. 'We can think that our belief patterns or our personalities are fixed, but actually neuroscience proves that the neurons in our brains can be rewired and we can build new neural pathways in the brain,' says Claire.

Understanding what our beliefs are about certain events is the first step to reframing and reprogramming the mind and changing our response. 'Looking at the model, you might find that an activating event happens quite frequently and the consequences are that you start shouting and can't think straight,' says Claire. 'Now you can ask yourself, "What's the belief system behind that? What's going on?" You might then think, "Am I overreacting? Am I overgeneralising? Am

I looking at the situation in a very finite way?" It's all about silencing that pesky little inner critic that makes us think we can't do things when we can.

'We create belief systems based on things that have happened to us,' Claire continues. 'In the past, a certain circumstance may have caused us humiliation, sadness or pain, and to protect us, the subconscious mind will create belief systems about certain situations even if they're not true.' This can affect our inner dialogue, making us over-catastrophise or overreact to certain situations. However, we can learn to change these mindsets.

Affirmations: Claire suggests using affirmations to reframe your internal dialogue: 'Have a think about what belief system you would need to develop to change your response to an activating event. Then think about affirmations you can say to encourage this.' This might be things such as repeating the phrase, 'I am a really interesting person. I am not boring,' or 'I am good at presenting. I am a powerful presence in a room.'

'The more you think a certain thought, the stronger the neural pathway becomes,' says Claire. This means the more you try and think in a different way, the more natural it will become. 'You can reframe and reprogramme the mind to choose your responses and learn to be more optimistic about certain events,' says Claire.

Use another ABC model: Another ABC model that is used in dialectical behaviour therapy (DBT) can also help us reframe our belief system and make us feel more optimistic. 'In this model, the "A" stands for "accumulate positive" experiences,' says Dr Tang. 'This can help us build up a positivity reservoir by doing things or keeping things around us that make us smile.' This could be anything from spending time with loved ones that make us feel great to reading a book you enjoy.

'The "B" is "build mastery",' says Dr Tang. 'Remember that *Friends* episode where Monica gets a bad restaurant review so she goes to a beginner's cooking class and is the best in the class? That is building mastery. Reminding yourself you're competent and good at things.'

The 'C', in this model, stands for 'cope ahead'. 'Again, by understanding what your activating events and beliefs are, you can create a clear crisis plan to make you feel safe in stressful situations,' says Dr Tang. 'This could be anything from having a fiddle toy in your bag you can play with when you get stressed to having an emergency teabag on hand.'

The Three R Method

It can be hard to anticipate when burnout will strike. People may feel varying levels of stress and tiredness, but when this heightens significantly, we often don't notice until it's too late. A long, gradual phenomenon, there are plenty of things you can do to prevent burnout from reaching its most intense point. One technique recommended by psychologists to manage and prevent burnout is the 'three R' approach. 'Burnout happens when our stress response continues for a long period of time, which leads to exhaustion,' explains Dr Tang. 'The three R technique helps you deal with stress responses as they arrive.'

The three Rs used in the method to prevent and deal with burnout are: recognise, reverse and resilience. Each of these three steps can help people deal with different stages of stress. 'Think of your stress response like an elastic band being stretched – burnout is the band snapping,' Dr Tang says. 'Prevention is really important because we need to build up our emotional strength just as we build up our physical strength,' she continues. 'Dealing with emotional issues at the point of crisis is not very effective.' The three R method can help you deal with each stage of stress, so you can build up a toolkit to deal with burnout in the long term. Here, Dr Tang breaks down the method simply to help you learn how to use it.

Step 1: Recognise

The first step of the three R method is learning to recognise when your body is stressed. 'It's OK to feel a stress response as long as you recognise it,' Dr Tang says. By recognising your stress, you can figure out what's triggering it and try to deal with that trigger head-on.

To help you learn to recognise when you're stressed, Dr Tang recommends doing regular body scans, either at the beginning or at the end of the day. 'To do a body scan, tense and relax each part of your body one by one,' she says. This will help you understand what your body feels like when it is stressed, so you can recognise that in other situations (for a full guided body scan, see page 247). She also suggests doing regular breathing practices to keep track of how you're feeling and to understand how your breathing is affected when you are stressed.

Step 2: Reverse

If you haven't been able to recognise your stress and deal with it before it becomes an issue, the next step is to try and remove that stress from your life while it's happening. 'Most of us overthink while we're stressed, so trying to stop ourselves from getting carried away with our thoughts is a good way to deal with stress,' Dr Tang says.

'Ask yourself what you can do to stop yourself feeling stressed, because taking action will stop your thoughts from spiralling. Our brains and our bodies are really adaptive, so unless we push them too far, you can always reverse your neuropathways.'

The action you take might be sending an email to the person who is causing you stress, or putting a plan in place so you know the thing that is stressing you out won't be a long-term issue. Figure out what it is that will allow you to calm down and find ways to try and do that, to avoid a prolonged stress response leading to burnout.

Step 3: Resilience

According to Dr Tang, resilience to stress is something you should try and build up all the time to prevent burnout. This is particularly important after you've dealt with a stressful situation. 'Building resilience isn't about how quickly or easily your stress response is triggered – it's about how long it takes you to calm down from it,' Dr Tang says.

To help you improve the ways you deal with stress and stop you from reaching the point of burnout, Dr Tang recommends practising mindfulness techniques (see pages 141–2), as well as meditation, affirmations and breathing techniques, so you have tools available for the next time you feel stressed.

'It's also important to stop taking on other people's stress and try to surround yourself with positive people who make you feel good,' Dr Tang continues. 'Try to change your approach to life to one of gratitude and try some gratitude practices. You can't feel stressed while you feel grateful.'

When stress is useful, and how to harness it

by Ben Ramalingam

Ben Ramalingam is the director of strategy and innovation at the British Red Cross, the latest stop on a career journey that has seen him advise the United Nations, NGOs and many national governments on human rights issues and disaster response. In some of the world's most high-pressure situations, he has seen people innovate, problem-solve and collaborate under incredible stress, which led him to write his book Upshift: Turning Pressure into Performance and Crisis into Creativity. *Here, he shares the things he's learned about stress that just might change the way you look at it.*

Stress can be a creative force

'I started working in disaster response about twenty years ago, during the Indian tsunami in 2004. I went on to work on the Pakistan floods, electoral violence in Kenya, the Nepal earthquake, Ebola outbreaks and much more. Through all of this work, I was really struck by that old phrase, "Necessity is the mother of invention" – I realised I thought it was actually a bit of a lie. Because in the most high-pressure situations, in extreme necessity, what most people did was buckle down. They were much more likely to reach for convention, doing what has always been done, rather than the risk of the new.

'But what I identified was that despite this, there was always a small number of people who seemed to actually use the pressure, and use the crisis, to trigger their creative responses and jump into action. They did novel and original things, and I became really interested in who these people were and why they were able to do what they did. I saw that when they came up with these brilliant ideas in response to a disaster, the ripple effects were enormous – the ideas would be shared widely and make a real positive difference to people's lives.

'So I started looking at the ingredients for these inventive moments in the face of lots of stressors. I started poking around in other areas; firstly, jobs that are related to disaster response, like ambulance work and police work and emergency surgery. But then I widened my net, looking at people who worked in the performing arts, [and] single parents on low incomes who were having to make it work with multiple kids. I identified that this stress-response skill was applicable in every walk of human life, really, from commuting to space travel, and if more of us could learn to harness it, that could be really transformative.'

Our perception is powerful

'If the first pandemic was Covid, I'd say the secondary pandemic was stress and anxiety. We had a huge lack of understanding about what was going on and what was going to happen to us from day to day. People were angry, people were upset, we were worried about relatives, ourselves, our livelihoods, and it pushed us to this point of collective stress that I think we're kind of still in. So understandably, we've become quite scared of stress. Our tendency, therefore, is to run away from it.

'But natural as it is, I think being scared of stress is actually a big problem, because we keep running away from it and trying to minimise it rather than looking it in the eye. I'll give a very specific example, based on research. In 1998, there was a large-scale US study which asked 30,000 adults across the country about their stress levels and their perception of stress. They were asked two things: How stressed are you? And how harmful do you think stress is to your health? They then assessed them again eight years later.

'What researchers found was that the people who were exposed to large amounts of stress *and* viewed stress as harmful had a forty-three per cent higher risk of dying than people who viewed stress as more neutral or just a part of life. The people with more positive perceptions of stress had the lowest risk of death out of all the people in the study, even lower than those who hardly experienced any stress at all. That's how powerful perception can be.

'In another study, researchers looked at stimulation in the workplace. They found that as we get older, we tend to gravitate towards jobs that are less pressured and have lower levels of challenge and stimulation, which at face value seems like an obvious thing to do, right? We want to look after our health and have an easy lead-up to retirement; we assume that seeking out less complex and stressful tasks is a good move. But actually, this diminishes our mental and biological wellbeing. The study found that the people who continued to have more stimulating and engaging everyday tasks, and even some stress, actually lived longer, had better mental performance and felt better about themselves. Again, it was a signifier that our attitude of always trying to run away from stressors and pressure is not necessarily good for us.'

Two exercises to help you reframe stress

Pressure drills
'It's like a fire drill for your mind. Once a week, imagine yourself in a specific stressful situation, whether that's at work, at home, with a certain difficult person in your life – anything at all that you might be anticipating. Imagine how you would typically deal with it, letting your mind flow, not thinking about it too much – lots of us do this naturally when we're worrying anyway. But then stop, press rewind, and ask yourself: what could I do differently to make that situation less stressful, if it happens?

'For example, I used to be so nervous about talking in public that my throat would almost close up and I'd lose my voice, and every time, I'd worry about that happening again. Then I started hitting rewind and thinking, what if I just admitted to that 1,000-strong audience that I was nervous? Because as soon as you are vulnerable with people, they tend to be on your side, they're rooting for you, and that is immediately calming. I did exactly what I'd imagined in my pressure drill the next time I had to speak, and it went well.'

After-pressure review
'Following a situation where we're under stress, we often tell ourselves, "Oh, I didn't do well, which obviously means I just

don't perform well under pressure", and this becomes a self-fulfilling thing. After-pressure reviewing is an adaptation of a tool that was developed by the US army, and it consists of asking yourself four questions:

- *What was supposed to happen?*
- *What actually happened?*
- *Why was there a difference?*
- *What am I going to do differently next time?*

'It sounds really simple, but if you ask yourself these questions every time you find yourself under stress and you felt you didn't perform as well because of it, this allows you to use it as a learning opportunity and reduce the stress around it moving forward. It becomes a really useful tool for grounding yourself, learning and then letting go.'

11. This chapter will change the way you rest

Tired? Thought so. As a generation, despite having every time-saving invention known to woman, we are still the most overwhelmed, burned out and downright knackered group of people the world has ever seen. Most modern technology, from the washer-dryer to the mobile phone, was invented to make our lives more efficient and allow us to do more with less effort. So why are we so exhausted? How did we get here, to a moment in time that market research leaders Mintel have dubbed 'the Year of Hyper Fatigue'?

One answer is that our minds are overrun with information. We have access to twenty-four-hour rolling news from every corner of the globe, as well as insight into the daily lives of every person we've ever met via social media. We're in WhatsApp groups and on Zoom calls and in Slack chats at all hours of the day. All of this can keep us in a state of hypervigilance that makes it difficult to switch off, let alone get proper rest; at any moment, there might be the ping of a message or a breaking news story or a work project that crops up to disturb our peace.

The statistics are consistent, loud and clear. According to a YouGov poll from 2022, one in eight Britons feel tired *all* the time, while a quarter of us feel tired most of the time. Generally, women are more tired than men: sixty-one per cent of us say we feel tired when we wake up, even after a full night's sleep, while just forty-nine per cent of men say the same. Something has gone seriously wrong with our relationship to rest, and as women we're suffering exponentially.

So rest is a feminist issue, but you already knew that. Women do several extra hours of domestic, caring and even emotional labour per day on average compared with men – often alongside our jobs – which inevitably is a huge drain on our physical and mental energy. It also leaves us with far less time to do the things that regenerate and reinvigorate us: not just sleep, but things like socialising, self-care and fun for fun's sake, which are all vital forms of downtime.

It's easy to assume that getting more, or better quality, sleep is the sole key to feeling less tired and more alert, but the truth is it's just a small part of the puzzle. This is the realisation that Dr Saundra Dalton-Smith came to when she decided to write her seminal book *Sacred Rest: Recover Your Life, Renew Your Energy, Restore Your Sanity*, which talks about the seven different forms of rest she believes we need to feel truly energised and able to live life to the full.

A quick guide to Dr Dalton-Smith's seven forms of rest

Physical rest

Sleeping and napping are the passive forms of physical rest, while restorative physical activity, such as yoga, stretching, massage and physiotherapy, is the active form.

Mental rest

Brain fog, difficulty completing a thought and lack of concentration are all signs you need mental rest. Giving your brain a break can come in the form of daydreaming, jotting down your thoughts in a notepad or practising mindfulness.

Sensory rest

We live in a world flush with sensory stimulants, from bright lights and flashing notifications to noisy roads. Being intentional about resting some of your senses can look like turning off your electronic devices for stretches of time, closing your eyes for a few moments during the working day, or even trying a sensory-deprivation therapy like a flotation tank.

Creative rest

We all need to solve problems and come up with fresh ideas in various areas of our lives, but when we're run down, the ability to do this can feel a million miles away. Creative rest is about reinvigorating your sense of wonder and seeing the world with fresh eyes. Brand-new experiences like travel can help, but it doesn't have to take that much time and money; you can also achieve creative rest by surrounding yourself with beauty at an art gallery or a garden.

Emotional rest

This just means authenticity and honesty. There is a release in speaking your truth when you're not feeling great, rather than expending energy trying to seem fine or mask your real emotions.

Social rest

We all know the difference between the relationships that buoy us and the ones that deplete us; it's time to pay that dichotomy more attention, because certain people could be sapping your life force. Positive, supportive and uplifting interactions always renew us – seek them out.

Spiritual rest

You don't necessarily need to believe in a higher power to get spiritual rest, it's simply about being able to connect to something bigger than yourself and your daily life, to tap into the power of community.

*

Dr Dalton-Smith's work has kicked off a crucial conversation about how our approach to modern fatigue might need to be more holistic than we once thought; there may be more to looking after ourselves than just getting our eight hours of sleep every night. So while we wish you sweet dreams, we also want you to consider these fresh ways of thinking about rest, downtime and regeneration. Your body and mind will thank you for it.

First things first, why are we so tired?

Research shows that the average British person spends seven and a half years of their life feeling tired, which is more than twenty hours per week. Feeling tired can have a huge effect on your quality of life. It can dictate your mood, how well you perform at work, your ability to exercise, and your capacity to do all the other things you enjoy. If you've already tried every pillow spray, white-noise playlist and lavender candle out there, perhaps it's time to consider whether you're really getting what you need from your resting time. Here, Dr Lindsay Browning, a chartered psychologist, sleep expert and the founder of clinic and consultancy Trouble Sleeping, outlines eight common reasons that might explain why you feel tired and how to deal with them.

1. You're not getting the right amount of sleep

According to Dr Browning, most people need between seven and nine hours sleep each night, although a small percentage of people will need more or less than this. 'If you're not getting the amount of sleep you need, you're going to be sleep-deprived,' says Dr Browning.

In order to figure out if you're getting the right amount of sleep, Dr Browning recommends taking note of how you feel around fifteen to twenty minutes after waking up. 'If you're getting between seven and nine hours and you feel refreshed after you wake up and as though you have enough energy throughout the day, then that's the right amount of sleep for you,' she advises. You can trial different amounts of sleep to see which quantity allows you to feel most refreshed.

However, the way you feel when you first wake up is not a good indicator of whether you have slept well or if you've had enough sleep, Dr Browning stresses. 'This is all dependent on which point during your sleep cycle you've woken up,' she explains, and this shouldn't affect your sleep quality or tiredness levels in the long term.

If you're getting significantly less than seven hours or significantly more than nine hours of sleep each night, Dr Browning suggests making sure that this amount is actually right for you and trialling getting between seven and nine hours to see how you feel. 'If you do need ten to eleven hours of sleep, maybe there is something else going on, like bad sleep quality or a health issue,' she says. 'And if you're getting a lot less than seven hours' sleep, look at your lifestyle and make sure that you're not just running on adrenaline.'

2. Your lifestyle doesn't suit your chronotype

'Strictly speaking, the hours of the day in which you sleep don't really matter,' Dr Browning says, explaining that our bodies are able to adapt to different time zones fairly easily. This means that as long as your sleep pattern is consistent, the hours during which sleep takes place are not that important.

However, your chronotype may be influencing your sleep. In the past, chronotypes were typically thought to dictate whether you were a lark (someone who tends to prefer going to sleep earlier and waking up earlier) or an owl (people who tend to get more alert as the day goes on and want to go to bed later and wake up later). However, new ideas about a wider range of chronotypes have recently made their way into the mainstream (more on this later).

Unfortunately, lifestyle factors, like work and family commitments, often mean you can't be guided by your chronotype as much as you'd like to be. 'The most beneficial thing you can do, in this case, is have a regular bedtime and a regular wake time,' Dr Browning says, adding that larks and owls tend to change their sleeping routines significantly on the weekends, which can make them feel more tired during the week.

3. You're not getting outside enough

'Exposure to daylight is really important for our circadian rhythm,' Dr Browning says. 'When we see the sun, it helps the brain know what time it is.' Particularly with the shift towards remote working, a lot of people aren't getting out the house enough, which could be affecting how tired you feel. 'Sitting by a window is good, but getting outside is far more effective – try and get outside every day for a walk, ideally in the morning,' Dr Browning recommends.

4. You're consuming too much caffeine

We hear you sighing. It's probably not what you want to hear – especially if it's the only thing that peps you up in the morning – but drinking too many caffeinated drinks can negatively impact your sleep and cause you to feel more tired during the day. 'You'll also have regular dips that will make you feel extra sluggish when caffeine wears off,' Dr Browning says. You don't have to cut out caffeine altogether, but Dr Browning recommends not drinking it after 3pm apart from in exceptional circumstances, and also suggests that you significantly reduce your intake to see if this helps you feel more energised.

5. You're not getting what you need from your diet

Diet has a huge effect on energy levels and what you're eating could be making you feel more tired. 'Things like low iron levels and vitamin D deficiencies can cause fatigue,' Dr Browning says, explaining that it's a good idea to get tested for deficiencies if you think you are getting enough sleep but you still feel tired all the time.

'Eating less fatty, starchy foods can help generally,' Dr Browning says, explaining that a balanced diet that suits you is one of the things that will boost your energy the most. 'Foods that are high in carbohydrates and fat, especially those that are processed, tend to make you feel sluggish,' she adds. That slump after lunch is rarely a coincidence.

6. You're not moving your body enough

'You might think exercise would make you feel more tired but, actually, it helps to increase your long-term stamina and makes you feel healthier and happier,' Dr Browning says. Implementing a regular exercise routine, even if it's just something low impact like walking, is guaranteed to help you feel more energised, while also improving your sleep quality. A physically tired body tends to mean a quieter mind and a deeper sleep, so it's worth prioritising.

7. You're struggling with your mental health

People struggling with their mental health often feel drained and exhausted, according to Dr Browning, so it's worth considering where you're at mentally. 'You might not have a lot of motivation to be awake if you're suffering from low mood, for example, which might make you feel sluggish and sleepy,' she explains. 'Emotional health is really important, and if you're struggling, it's important to speak to a professional.' Try not to beat yourself up about lacking energy and motivation in this situation – it's completely understandable and normal.

8. You have an undiagnosed health issue

If your tiredness is severe and none of the above explanations feel relevant for you, you may be struggling with a sleep-specific health issue. There are many health issues that are specific to sleep, like sleep apnoea and chronic fatigue. If you're concerned, your first port of call should be your GP. Long Covid has also been known to cause increased tiredness, so if you have been diagnosed with Covid-19 at any point since the pandemic began, it's worth speaking to your doctor about how this might have impacted your tiredness levels, Dr Browning advises. Although many of us are used to doing our best with the energy we've got, no one should have to go through life feeling permanently tired.

So, what's your chronotype? Why you may not be an owl or a lark

Our sleeping patterns and the way we should sleep to feel most rested can vary dramatically from person to person, and they are usually genetically preconditioned – so if you're a person who struggles to wake up early no matter how long you've been in bed, that's not necessarily a failing, it's just the way you are. Chronotypes are a classification system that helps sort us into various sleep categories based on our circadian rhythms or 'body clocks', and for a long time we talked about people either being night owls or morning larks. But Dr Michael Breus, aka the Sleep Doctor, more recently identified four chronotypes that his clients seemed to fall into, each named after an animal with similar habits.

The bear

This is the most common chronotype, accounting for more than half of the population, and named after an animal that hunts throughout the day and sleeps solidly at night. Society is set up, by and large, for bears, with working hours that suit their circadian rhythms. If you're a bear, you rise and fall with the sun, spend most of the day awake and alert, and sleep for around eight hours each night. Typically, you will feel most productive in the morning and probably hit an afternoon slump after lunch at around 3pm.

> **APPLY IT:** *Try to do activities that will require the most physical energy, such as working out, in the morning while you feel the most refreshed. As you go through the day, you'll find it becomes harder and harder to motivate yourself.*

The lion

Around fifteen per cent of us are natural lions, like the animal that hunts in the morning. It means you're an early-to-rise and early-to-bed kind of person, have a natural tendency towards healthy routines, and normally wake up feeling energised. You're at your best between 7am and 12pm, but may feel exhausted and have difficulty focusing by the time afternoon rolls around.

> **APPLY IT:** *When you feel that natural dip around lunchtime, try not to ignore it by scrolling your phone, and don't try to push through it by working. Instead, get outside, go for a walk or do some stretches; something that will help you reset and give your brain a bit of a break, rather than pushing you further into an afternoon slump.*

The wolf

Another fifteen per cent of the population are wolves, also known as night owls. You might have trouble waking up in the morning no matter how long you've slept, but find yourself alert, creative and sociable in the evening when others are winding down. Your productivity power hours tend to be around the end of the typical working day.

> **APPLY IT:** *Although your alertness will start peaking around 6–7pm, making it a good time to get intense work done or go for a run, try to be in bed by midnight. This is when your body will start to naturally wind down, but it means you'll still be able to get up for a standard working day without compromising on your sleep.*

The dolphin

The final chronotype, which accounts for around ten per cent of people, gets its namesake from an animal that is a unihemispheric sleeper, meaning that they only ever sleep with one half of their brain at a time while the other half is still active. Dolphin chronotypes may feel tired all day, but then struggle to fall asleep and stay asleep all night, when you become full of restless energy. You're likely to be sensitive to external stimuli such as light and sound, so you're easily woken up during the night, too.

> **APPLY IT:** Try keeping a worry journal by your bedside that will help you get incessant thoughts out of your head and down on paper before bedtime. Research has shown that taking a few moments to write down your to-do list for the next day can actually help you fall asleep quicker.

One of those sound familiar? It's worth figuring out what your body's natural tendencies are when it comes to resting time and alertness, and trying to adjust your daily life (as much as possible) to ensure you're not constantly battling against it.

CBT methods to help you sleep better

There's nothing more frustrating than tossing and turning in bed, not being able to drift off. But beyond this frustration, not getting the amount of shut-eye you need can also impact your health, with

tiredness causing increased stress and difficulty concentrating.
If you're having trouble sleeping night after night and feel like
you've tried everything to nod off, from reducing your caffeine
intake to cutting out screen time in the evening, then experimenting
with some more focused techniques could help improve your sleep.
Cognitive behavioural therapy is commonly used to help treat mental
health issues like anxiety and depression, but it can also be used to
help with sleeplessness.

   'Cognitive behavioural therapy for insomnia (CBT-I) works best
when tailored towards a specific person,' says Ana Brito, certified
somnologist and co-found of Somnissimo. There are a huge number of
tools from CBT-I that you can try to figure out which ones work best
for you. These tools are useful for anyone struggling with their sleep,
even though they're generally used, in a medical setting, for those
struggling with insomnia.

Stimulus control

'If you wake up in the middle of the night or you're struggling to fall
asleep for more than twenty minutes, get out of bed,' Brito says. 'Go
and get a glass of water, do some meditation, walk around your living
room.' Stimulus control trains your mind and body so that going to
bed means going to sleep via learned association. Getting out of bed
when you can't sleep is a good way to reinforce this, as you want to
maintain that connection between your bed and sleep, and avoid
associating your bed with sleeplessness. When you are up and about,
though, you should keep your lights dim so you're not interrupted by
too much light exposure.

Progressive muscle relaxation (PMR)

'Progressive muscle relaxation involves contracting and relaxing different muscle groups one by one, usually accompanied by guided meditation,' Brito explains. This technique will help you to feel more physically and mentally relaxed, as it not only sends the body signals to calm down, but it also keeps your mind occupied. You should spend about ten to fifteen minutes practising PMR, tensing each muscle for a few seconds and then slowly relaxing them for about twenty to thirty seconds. You can either start at the top or the bottom of your body and make your way through all your major muscle groups.

Thought records

'During the day, write down your negative thoughts and worries on a piece of paper and try to find a solution or plan to address them,' Brito says. 'This will help to make sure that bedtime isn't the only quiet time of your day when negative thoughts will inevitably arise.' Write down your thoughts and what your next steps are to tackle the issues you're worrying about. When those thoughts come at night, you'll then know that you've already got a plan, and there's nothing you can do in that moment to help other than get a good rest. You can do your thought records at any point during the day, but it's crucial to take the time to do so before you're winding down for the night.

When sleep still won't come: everything you need to know about insomnia

Insomnia can be devastating. Writhing around in the dark can feel unnerving and lonely, not to mention exhausting when the morning finally arrives. When you're trapped in your own thoughts in the middle of the night, sleeplessness can be an isolating experience, but insomnia is actually extremely common. A third of the global population will suffer from sleep problems at some point in their lives, while ten per cent will be diagnosed with insomnia. During the pandemic, nearly two-thirds of people in a study by King's College London said their sleep quality had become worse.

In response, there's been a proliferation of apps, gadgets and self-help guides released in recent years, all aiming to get us sleeping better, but spending so much time tracking and worrying about our sleep could actually be making it worse.

'There's been a huge focus on sleep hygiene and the idea of "clean sleep",' says Stephanie Romiszewski, chief medical officer and sleep physiologist at Re:Sleep. The term 'orthosomnia' has even been coined to describe our obsession with getting the perfect night's sleep. 'But, just like "clean eating", "clean sleep" doesn't exist, and this focus on sleep actually leads to increased anxiety around it,' Stephanie says.

Stephanie believes we might not have such an insomnia epidemic if we were all properly educated about sleep. Last year, her research found that doctors studying undergraduate medical degrees were only given around an hour and a half of sleep education throughout their studies. 'Doctors don't understand sleep well because they don't get much education on it,' says Stephanie. 'This means the general public isn't educated on what sleep is and how it works, which means we start freaking out when we've got a sleep problem.' Here, Stephanie outlines what we really need to know about sleep and insomnia, including the mistakes we might be making in our daily routines that make it so difficult to drift off.

What is the definition of insomnia?

The textbook definition of insomnia and the symptoms a doctor will look for to diagnose it usually describe someone who has suffered from sleep disruption for at least three months, struggles with sleep more often than not in their week and whose lack of sleep affects how they function during the day.

However, Stephanie explains that insomnia can embody a whole host of different disrupted sleeping patterns. Sleep-onset insomnia, for example, is where someone struggles to get to sleep, while sleep-maintenance insomnia is when someone struggles to stay asleep during the night. 'There are many different variations,' says Stephanie. 'You might take hours to get to sleep. You might not have any problems getting to sleep, but then you wake in the night several times, or you just can't get back to sleep once you're awake in the middle of the night. It can even be a mixture of these things.'

What causes insomnia?

'It's very important to understand that to treat insomnia, you don't need to worry about the triggers,' says Stephanie. 'The things that directly cause insomnia are not necessarily the perpetuating factors.' Insomnia may be a symptom of something else, like stress, anxiety, depression, an illness, or a new medication. Stephanie explains it's completely normal to experience sleep problems due to these things. 'It's just your body trying to adapt to the new situation,' she says. However, when sleeping problems persist, it's important to look beyond the initial trigger and examine more closely how our behaviour influences our sleep instead.

The vicious cycle of sleep anxiety

'Sleep is becoming such a zeitgeisty area,' says Stephanie. 'We have books, apps and trackers telling us we need to sleep more and that if we don't, bad things will happen to us.' However, this only increases our urgency for sleep and we start to fear not sleeping. 'Then suddenly you've got anxiety about your sleep, and it's not just a sleep problem anymore – it's anxiety as well.'

Stephanie explains it can become an addiction to have a sleep problem: 'You become so obsessed with the little coping mechanisms you're given, and you start obsessing over all these things. The irony is, you end up creating more of a sleep problem than you had before. I see tens of thousands of people in my sleep clinic,' she continues. 'Most of them are just very anxious, stressed-out people who are creating the problem themselves. It's not their fault, it's the way that our society deals with sleep.'

The ultimate goal is to get to a place where sleep isn't a concern anymore. 'A good sleeper is defined by somebody who doesn't care about it,' says Stephanie. 'They might not sleep perfectly, because nobody sleeps eight hours every night, but they don't care. That is liberating.'

Overthinking sleep debt

When it comes to sleep, it's not an eye for an eye, explains Stephanie. 'If you lose four hours of sleep in a night, it doesn't mean your body needs to gain four hours of sleep.' When we try to make up for lack of sleep, it may lead us to go to bed earlier, lie in for longer or nap to recover the sleep we've lost the night before. All this does is disrupt your routine and make you more anxious, warns Stephanie. 'It's not that sleep debt doesn't exist,' she says. 'But it's something we don't have the power to change, so the best thing you can do is use that extra bit of sleep deprivation you've incurred to boost your sleep cycle, rather than try to increase your sleep.'

So, what can I do?

Stick to a routine

Creating a regulated sleep cycle by waking up at the same time every day is one of the best things you can do. Even if you haven't got as much sleep as you'd like the night before, getting out of bed at a set time helps build good sleeping habits. 'It might seem counterintuitive to get out of bed earlier if you've had a bad night's sleep,' says Stephanie, 'but if you keep waking up at the same time every day for long enough, I promise you, you will slowly start to become a morning person. You'll probably notice after several weeks of following that routine that you do start going to bed around about the same time and you won't have to force it.'

Rethink weekend lie-ins

You must factor weekends into your healthy sleep routine. 'A lot of people want to lie in on the weekends and not get as much sleep during the week,' says Stephanie. 'That is never going to work long term. If you're going to regulate your sleep so you start to go to bed naturally, it's important to try and wake up at the same time every day.'

Stick to your usual daytime habits

It's also important not to change your routine during the day. 'If you worry about getting extra sleep and let insomnia take over, you'll stop going to the gym, you'll stop seeing your friends late because you're worried it's going to eat into your sleep opportunity. You'll start obsessing over relaxation,' says Stephanie. 'The irony is, if you had changed nothing, if you'd kept going to the gym, moving around, seeing your friends and enjoying life, you'd find that your brain would happily start doing the work for you and would naturally make you sleepier.'

Build your sleep drive

When people try to compensate for lack of sleep, it can lead them to spend more time in bed to give their bodies more opportunity to sleep. 'The issue is when you've had sleep problems, you just teach your brain to dilute your sleep by doing this,' says Stephanie. 'If you spend ten hours in bed, your brain thinks it doesn't need to give you one block of sleep anymore. It thinks it can make you sleep for the first hour, wake up for the next hour and give you a disrupted night's sleep because you're in bed for so long. Then your body gets used to coping and compensating for lack of sleep.'

If this sounds like you, you may lack a strong sleep drive, meaning your body isn't signalling to your brain that you need a long period of deep rest. This, says Stephanie, is a scenario in which ditching a strict bedtime schedule can actually be helpful. 'Allow your body to build a strong sleep drive by only going to bed when you feel really tired,' says Stephanie. 'The longer you stay awake, the stronger your need to sleep is. If you're not able to sleep that's totally fine. It just means you need to spend more time awake in order to build that sleep drive.'

Don't rely on quick fixes

Looking for a quick fix to a sleep problem is often an instantaneous reaction when we start struggling to drift off. 'Wouldn't it be nice if your twenty-year sleep problem was fixed by buying a new mattress?' says Stephanie. 'But that cannot be.'

You can never change a routine you've habitually built, even one that's not making you feel good, with a quick fix. 'You need to dismantle it over time,' says Stephanie. 'So, while things like massage, sleeping pills and CBD oil can help with short-term sleep problems, longer-term issues need greater behavioural changes.'

Focus on light

As we discussed earlier, light is incredibly important for human beings – 'We are much more like plants than people realise,' says Stephanie – so it's important we use light to our advantage to help us wake up and get to sleep. 'You can trick your brain into being really awake in the mornings by exposing yourself to lots of bright light, even if you didn't get any sleep the night before,' Stephanie advises.

Instead of using coffee to try and stay awake, light is a much healthier alternative. Light also has the ability to repair your sleep. Using light differently in the evenings, like turning off overhead lights and reducing the brightness on our screens, can help prepare you for sleep. 'Starting your day off super bright and then, just like the sun going down, reducing the amount of light you're exposed to in the evening is very powerful,' says Stephanie.

How to beat brain fog when you didn't sleep well

The feeling of grogginess we get after a restless night can have a deep impact on us, according to Dr Sonia Khan, lead pharmacist at Medicine Direct. Dr Khan explains that grogginess occurs when 'the body can't carry out the essential maintenance that it's required to do every night. For individuals that do not fall into the later stages of sleep, this means that your brain effectively stays active all day and is unable to effectively process and store yesterday's events. In essence, your brain has not switched off from the previous day. Your body is also unable to repair any damaged cells and muscles to ensure there is enough energy in them for the following day.'

No matter how many sleep hacks you try, sometimes there's no escaping a disrupted night. Although we can't replace the hours of lost shut-eye, experts have determined that our bodies' responses to certain stimuli can lead to an increased feeling of alertness. Read on for three science-backed ways to fight the brain fog that follows a night of little sleep.

Practise yoga nidra

Pulling your yoga mat out after waking up from a long night of tossing and turning might seem counterproductive, but Risa Gabrielle, a certified sleep therapist, swears by this yoga practice and says, 'Thirty minutes of yoga nidra can feel like the equivalent of getting up to two more hours of sleep.'

Yoga nidra – or yogic sleep, as it's commonly known – is 'a deeply guided meditation that puts you in a hypnotic and hypnagogic (between sleep and rest) state'. Gabrielle says: 'It slows your brainwaves, so you are able to experience the restorative benefits of sleep while technically still being awake. And it helps you access the parasympathetic nervous system and relaxation response. Unlike taking a nap, you don't feel groggy when you finish a yoga nidra.' She advises using free guided yoga nidra sessions on YouTube or the Yoga Nidra Network.

Utilise intentional stressors

Not to be confused with mental or emotional stress, physical stress involves putting the body in a situation that 'positively stimulates adrenaline release'. Despite feeling tired and sleepy, putting your body through its paces with a short HIIT workout or a quick run can 'give you a burst of energy in the morning'.

If you're not huge on physical activity first thing in the morning, Gabrielle suggests taking a cold shower – start warm and then work your way to cold – or practising techniques such as Wim Hof (the combination of breathwork with cold therapy) or Tummo breathing (deep breathing and visualisation), which can elicit the same energy high. Gabrielle explains, 'The reason this works is that these are positive stressors that will increase adrenaline and cortisol levels – they'll certainly give you energy in the short term.'

For people who suffer with chronic sleeplessness disorders such as insomnia, the habitual practice of intentional stress has long-term benefits. Gabrielle says that over time, your brain starts to associate the stressor with the positive effect of boosted energy. She explains: 'What that does is it helps release dopamine and serotonin, which helps the body get more out of the adrenaline release. By marrying the adrenaline and cortisol spike with the feel good hormone dopamine, and the mood-stabilising hormone serotonin, these practices help you manage the stress response in your body in the long term.'

Get into the light

We already know that getting out into natural light can boost your mood. However, instead of saving your daylight hour for a relaxing lunchtime walk, when chasing an early energy boost, Gabrielle suggests you 'get outside within the first thirty to sixty minutes of waking up'.

Using this method to counteract the effects of bad sleep depends on timing 'the body's cortisol release so that it is strongest in the mornings. Getting this daylight also prevents a late shift in cortisol release – which correlates with anxiety, depression, insomnia.' She explains, 'The right amount of cortisol in the morning helps to improve focus, energy levels and learning.'

When it comes to light exposure, it's not just a matter of when but also of how much. Gabrielle specifies: 'On a sunny day, get outside for five to ten minutes; if it's overcast, ten to twenty minutes will do. If it's a particularly dull day, it takes about thirty minutes to get the right amount of daylight.'

How to *really* rest on holiday

The holiday: a concept as old and sacred as the working week itself, and a necessity that even big business sees as crucial to keeping its employees, if not happy, then able to keep on working well. No matter how much we enjoy our work, taking the time to put our feet up, spend time with loved ones or simply use our brains and bodies in a different way is vital to our long-term wellbeing. It can also give us a fresh perspective and renewed sense of purpose at work when it's time to return after a bit of distance and mental space. So why, according to a study by Timetastic, did 6 per cent of all workers not take their annual leave allowance?

Part of it, no doubt, is that lots of us are under too much pressure in our jobs today. Our workloads are so huge that we feel we can't step away, even for a few days, without things falling apart or a mountain piling up on our desks that will be so stressful it won't be worth the holiday at all. In some workplaces, too, there can be a toxic culture of presenteeism, meaning being seen to take time off will leave you feeling judged and like you're missing out on something important.

Even when we do manage to get away, we often feel like we can't fully immerse ourselves, that we still need to keep one eye on our working lives for all the reasons above. We all know how hard it is to separate work and play in an era when a 'per my last email' can be pinged into the palm of your hand, whether you're on a cable car in Courchevel or a massage bed in Bali. But our perpetual state of 'on'-ness is exactly why switching off on holiday is more vital to our health and happiness than ever.

Despite it being proven that taking time out from work and the stresses of everyday life boosts our productivity and contentment when we return, a study by the Institute of Leadership & Management found that more than sixty-four per cent of full-time workers read and respond to emails while on holiday, and seventy-three per cent feel more stressed than usual in the run-up to annual leave.

We tell ourselves if we just keep a hand in and try to keep on top of our work, then there'll be less panic once we return to our desks. But as tempting as it is to keep checking your email every time you see a notification, we need to make sure we're not only taking holidays, but switching off properly once we're on them so we feel fully rested when we get back. This is how to make the most of all the benefits leisure time has to offer.

The 5-step O-O-O checklist

1. Draw a line under work

Let's start with the hardest one, shall we? As more of us go freelance, juggle side hustles and buckle under the weight of our inboxes, a job can feel less like a nine-to-five and more like a lifestyle. But when it comes to taking a holiday, we have to be firm about stepping away from work – both with our colleagues and with ourselves. Tying up any loose ends, writing a to-do list for when you get back and ensuring everyone knows you're going away makes this ten times easier.

Treat the days before you head out of the office like the end of term: leave nothing half-written, half-baked or half-done. If you must, delegate the rest of the project you're working on to a colleague. There's nothing worse than having unfinished business hanging over your head while you're trying to chill out. It might mean staying an hour later on your last day, but it will make crafting that smug out-of-office email all the sweeter.

2. Tackle your to-do list

We're talking life admin here; that stuff that piles up when you're busy with work and more fun endeavours, so you keep kicking the can down the road until suddenly a stack of dry-cleaning, filing and fixing home appliances looms ominously over your precious annual leave. Pre-holiday is a perfect time for a to-do list cull – we recommend removing anything you've been putting off for more than a few weeks (it clearly isn't that important, the world won't fall apart) then tackling the rest with the enthusiasm

of a woman who has a poolside cocktail firmly in her sights.
Future-you will be very grateful.

3. Ask a friend to check on your home

Wondering whether you've turned off all the lights or are being
aggressively burgled at any given moment can take up a lot of
thinking time while on holiday, but there is a simple resource you
can tap up to mitigate these worries: your lovely friends. If you're
close with a neighbour, ideal – otherwise, ask a friend who lives
nearby if they mind checking on your home every couple of days
to put your mind at ease. They can water your plants while
they're at it!

4. Ditch the data

There is so much happening online every minute of every day
that we can feel like we're missing out if we don't check our
phones constantly. But being able to see where your friends are
planning to meet up for dinner or what your colleagues are
discussing on Slack is entirely useless when you're away,
and it'll trigger stress and distract you from the real-life
experiences at hand.

   Try doing without data and only using Wi-Fi for a short period
every day – removing the temptation to Instagram every holiday
moment in real time means you'll be more engaged with your
companions and less concerned with watching the likes and
comments roll in. Plus, looking through your pictures in the
evening and choosing what you want to share then can be a nice
way of reflecting on the day.

5. Soften the blow

With a bit of organisation, the existential dread that comes at the end of some time off can be nipped in the bud. Although we always want to make the most of our annual leave, planning to head straight into work the day after you get home is a recipe for early-onset holiday blues. Make sure you have at least half a day as a buffer, and book in a catch-up with friends or family or an activity you find calming, like going for a swim. Having something quick and tasty in the freezer and fresh bed linen ready for your return will make home all the more inviting, too. Now go forth and holiday better.

12. How to biohack your way back from burnout

by Charlène Gisèle

Charlène Gisèle is a coach and speaker who pivoted careers after she suffered serious stress-related burnout while working as a lawyer in London. Although her career kept reaching new heights, she realised the long hours and high pressure were affecting her health. She decided it was time to take a break, travel the world and learn how to help others avoid career-driven burnout. Here, she shares the biohacking and body-first tools she's sharpened along the way.

My time working in the City was stressful and my days were fully packed, not to mention my evenings and weekends. I was really burning the candle at both ends, and eventually I realised that it was all a bit much and my mental and physical health was suffering.

So I took a break. I went on a global adventure – a healing journey, if you like – and when I came back I pivoted to a career that would allow me to help others who had been through career-driven burnout. I'm passionate about sharing the tools that not only saved me, but have helped so many of my clients. And now I'd like to share them with you.

What is biohacking?

You might have heard the term 'biohacking' and wondered what it meant. It's a term that comes from Silicon Valley and the idea of 'hacking' your own biology. It's really about optimising the external factors around you but also optimising your own biology and reaching a state of peak performance at a physical, cognitive and emotional level. It's being the best person you can be. It's adding years to your life, but also adding life to your years.

So how does this relate to burnout? Burnout is characterised by an accumulation of chronic stress, fatigue and feeling overwhelmed on both a physical and emotional level. If you look after your biology and your physiology, and take care of your body and your emotional and psychological state, you are a lot less likely to go into a full burnout.

Biohacking is very wide and very diverse. You might have seen some extreme examples on TV: somebody altering their DNA with a CRISPR injection or putting chips into their forearms. Don't worry – no chips involved here. Although you can have a lot of fancy tech, I am a firm believer that the most powerful biohacks are the ones that stay with you at all times. The ones that are already built in, are already part of you. The first one is your breath, and the second one is your brain. When you biohack these two things, you are guaranteed to kiss career-driven burnout goodbye.

Although biohacking is an umbrella term for a wide range of different activities, there is some common ground. It's about tracking and measuring, and regaining control over your body and performance. In the biohacking community, we often say, 'If you want to hack it, you have to track it.'

Another aspect of biohacking is this incredible incorporation of ancestral wisdom. Things like intermittent fasting, meditation, forest bathing and spending time in nature are all ancestral pearls of wisdom that come back to the practise of biohacking.

Here, we're going to cover biohacking your breathing patterns as well as your brain. When you learn how to tap in to your physiological levers, you can optimise your sense of concentration, focus and performance, and that is the ultimate antidote to career burnout.

Part one: Biohack your breath

The first thing I want to invite you to biohack is your breathing patterns. Why? Because your breath is always with you. No excuses — you take it to work every day, you do it all night. In fact, it is the one thing that you do the most and think of the least. We breathe in and out between 20,000 and 23,000 times a day. How many of those breaths, today, do you think you took consciously?

What does breathing consciously even mean?

It means breathing with a sense of full awareness of the fact that you are breathing. What does it look like? Well, close your eyes and take a moment to inhale and exhale. You will have a lot of different thoughts coming into your mind in this moment; try to treat those thoughts like you might treat a wild puppy. You know it's there, but you're choosing not to entertain it.

What is extraordinary is we now live in the safest time in human history, with no big predators and fewer hostile environments to navigate. We are more stressed than ever before. Breathing is the antidote to stress if you know how to do it well and you build an aware breathing practice. Start with baby steps, very small changes. Of course, you could challenge yourself to do thirty minutes of breathwork right away, but is that realistic for you to commit to doing for the rest of your life? I am a firm believer in the power of incremental changes, because when you commit to doing something every day in small doses, and continue doing it consistently, at the end of the year those small doses compound, and that's where big changes happen.

Breathing and the nervous system

I want to give you a little introduction to the connection between breathing and your nervous system. This is where science meets yogic tradition. We have a nervous system called the autonomic system and this is what drives all the beautiful things that happen in your body without your having to command it – for example, your heartbeat, your digestion and, of course, your breathing. But here's the thing: the autonomic system becomes very much dysregulated when you live a high-stress life and are on the cusp of going into a full career-driven burnout.

The autonomic system is divided into two states. One of them is the sympathetic nervous system, responsible for your 'fight or flight' response. That might look something like this: you feel very stressed, your breathing becomes shallow and you'll most likely breathe through your mouth and from your chest, and your shoulders will be tense. Instead you want to activate the parasympathetic nervous system, which is responsible for the 'rest and digest' state.

Now the incredible thing about modulating your breathing pattern is that it is the most direct pathway into your parasympathetic nervous system. Yes, by breathing differently, you can tap into your 'rest and digest' state. How wonderful is that? And it's something that's readily available to you, wherever you are, whatever you do. It is, in fact, your new superpower.

The physiological sigh

There's an incredible type of breathwork modality that you can start now. It's called the physiological sigh, and it goes something like this: two short, sharp inhales through your nose, followed by an exhale through your mouth. Interestingly, if you have a pet, a young child or a baby, you might have noticed that they naturally do this. When a child is sobbing and trying to calm themselves down, they will often inhale twice quickly before letting the breath go instinctively. You might have seen a grown adult having a panic attack and doing this too. It is already built in to our biology as a tool for calming the body, but you can deploy it whenever necessary to settle anxiety.

The anatomy of a full breath

Let's talk about your nose and your mouth. Do you know where you inhale from? If you're faced with anxiety or stress, you're probably breathing through your mouth, but we are meant to inhale through our noses. The nose is designed to filter and warm the air that we breathe in, so it is absolutely vital that you watch out for mouth-breathing, otherwise you could be prolonging feelings of anxiety.

Now, turn your focus to how many breaths you take in a minute. Have you ever tracked it? Grab your watch or your phone and set a one-minute timer, then start counting. Every time you inhale and exhale counts as one breath. Keep a tally without modulating your natural breathing pattern. On average, adults take between ten and sixteen breaths per minute, but please don't worry if yours is higher than that. If it's in the low twenties, for example, it could simply mean that it would be a great idea for you to start doing calming breathwork because your stress levels are up. Be kind to yourself. And if you're a trained athlete or you already do a lot of breathwork, it might be in single digits. Either way, you're perfect where you are, this is simply intended to spark a curiosity about improving your breathing patterns. And this is what the heart of biohacking truly is: to be more aware of your body so that you can work towards being the most optimised version of yourself. Why wouldn't you want to be that?

Belly-breathing and breath modulation

These are two very simple techniques to bring yourself down to a state of instant relaxation. Next time you get anxious thoughts or your pulse is raised because you saw an email pop up or you have a meeting you feel nervous about, tap in to these techniques to self-soothe and engage the parasympathetic nervous system.

Belly-breathing

- Place your right hand on your belly.
- Take a full inhale through your nose and let your belly expand and rise.
- Fully exhale through your mouth, bringing your navel back towards your spine.
- Keep it slow and continuous for a minute or two.

Breath modulation

The second technique is one I learned in India from a brilliant breathwork master before I became a breathwork teacher myself, and it is also very simple yet powerful. It's about modulation of your inhale and your exhale. Our exhale slows down our heart rate, while our inhale elevates it, so what are we going to do to feel more relaxed? We're going to exhale for longer than we inhale.

- Inhale for three counts.
- Exhale for six counts.
- Repeat until you feel calmer and your body is more relaxed.

Breathing and the immune system

Breathing is one of the best preventative medicines to boost your immunity. Your immune system is your in-built protection mechanism against viruses and bacteria. Immunity is very closely linked to our lymph system, which transports all the little white blood cells that help us fight infection. But the lymph system, unlike the blood system, which is powered by the heart, does not have a pump. Movement pumps the lymphatic system, but how do you move enough to power it when you're spending eight hours a day at your desk working on a computer screen?

This is the mindset shift we could all benefit from: breathing is moving. Breath is movement. And by breathing optimally and efficiently, you will be creating a wider range of motion with the movement of your diaphragm, and you will give your body an extra boost of movement. Many people are unavoidably deskbound for a few hours each day, with those of us working in corporate jobs having to spend a lot of time sitting down.

Now, biohackers love to talk about 'mitochondrial health'. It means wellness on a cellular level, and one of the best ways to boost it is to improve your breathing technique, because it will take more oxygen into your cells. Boost your mitochondrial health, boost your immunity, and boost your overall health and wellbeing.

Box breathing

Now that you understand the mechanism of breathing a little better, I want to give you the ultimate biohacking starter pack when it comes to adopting a breathwork practice. It's a technique called box breathing that's been used by yogis for thousands of years and is also used by elite special forces and Navy SEALs. Not only does it help you to boost your peak performance at a physical level, but it also boosts your mental acuity. This is how it works:

- Close your eyes and imagine drawing a box in the air.
- Inhale for five counts while you draw the first line of the box.
- Hold your breath for five counts while you draw the second line.
- Exhale for five counts while you draw the third line.
- Hold your breath for five counts while you complete the box.
- Repeat for four rounds.

The best time to do this box-breathing technique is either when you wake up in the morning or just before you go to sleep, or anytime you come up against a particular stress trigger such as a difficult conversation. Do this practice to bring yourself into a state of calm and clarity.

Part two: Biohack your brain

The second element of biohacking that can help avoid, prevent and overcome burnout is to do with the control centre of your body: the brain. I'm particularly passionate about this topic. As a former lawyer, I like the idea of 'brainpower'. But we need to master the art of working smart, not necessarily working hard. There are five key hacks that can help you get your brain into gear for peak performance at work.

1. Single focus and the flow state

Let's talk about the life lots of us are living now. Constant distraction is everywhere because your attention has become the world's favourite commodity. All the apps on your phone, the notifications, the thousands of shows crying out from your smart TV – everything is seeking your attention. How do we regain power over our attention? By becoming masterful at single focus.

It might be a difficult one at first, but the first step is to remove your phone from your immediate vicinity. I really mean it. Whatever task you have in front of you that does not involve your phone, focus on that task and that task only. If you have an email that is important that you need to respond to, close all those unnecessary tabs, turn off those notifications, put your phone in a drawer (few of us have the willpower to not look at it if it's right there in front of us) and really focus on what you are doing in that moment. Not only will this skyrocket your productivity and efficiency, but it will also preserve your energy. We think that we can multitask, but multitasking is an illusion. What you're doing when you're multitasking is doing two things at a mediocre level. Do we want mediocre? No, we want outstanding. And if your attention is outstanding, your output is going to be outstanding.

Single focus is one of the best tools for getting you into a flow state: a state where you can perform your best but also feel your best. You might have heard it described by athletes, entrepreneurs or creatives as being 'in the zone' – and it's a thing, it's been backed up by science. Being in the zone is when all your senses are heightened.

You feel like your vision is sharper, your focus is undivided, and you're performing at your peak. Can you live life in a continuous flow state? No, but what your can do is learn a blueprint to help you get into this state quickly, so you can spend as much time as possible in it during your working hours. That's where all your creation, original thought and mastery will come through.

So now you know what a flow state looks like, you can set yourself up for success. Remove any potential distractions – as mentioned, phones are a big one – but also people. I mean that in the nicest possible way, but if you're working from home and you have a spouse or a loved one in the same space, do let them know that you're going into the zone and that for an hour, you are not to be distracted. The irony is, this is also the best way for you to be able to give your loved one your full attention; this skill is not only applicable to your career, but also to your relationships. You will be better at anything you do, because you are able to give that one thing or that one person your full, undivided attention.

Remember, attention is what everybody is trying to get out of you all the time – reclaim it. Use it to your advantage and become a master single-tasker.

2. Hacking stress

The second way to biohack your brain is linked to productivity and management skills. We often think that we should 'manage' our stress, but I'd invite you to reframe that. Manage your time instead. Become an excellent planner. This is how . . .

Set 'staircase' goals

First of all, you need to set goals. The key to setting a goal is that it needs to be crystal clear and as specific as possible, and it needs to be achievable. Bite-sized goals are best, because if you set yourself huge, vague goals like 'get a promotion', it's easy to feel overwhelmed or unmotivated to try and chase it because you're not clear what the next steps are. The third important thing to bear in mind when setting a goal is that it should be trackable – remember that biohacking mantra, 'If you want to hack it, you have to track it'.

There's a little tool you can use to feel less overwhelmed and clearer on how to set your goals effectively. It's a technique that in coaching we call 'the staircase'. Imagine a classic staircase, where you're standing at the bottom on the ground floor, looking up at the first floor. Now the feeling of overwhelm might come because you think you're going to have to jump from the ground floor to the first floor in one big leap, but of course you can't do that. And that stress of looking at all these big goals over days, weeks and months might build up and edge you towards burnout, which we want to avoid.

So, when we're on the metaphorical ground floor, we need to take it one stair at a time. Break down a big goal into a set of smaller steps, and don't move up a stair until the one you're on is fully complete. Keep it bite-sized and focus on progression. Nobody ever jumped up an entire staircase without an injury.

Start with a full cup

As part of your planning, you not only need to have clear goals but clear timelines. You might have some resistance to what I'm about to say, but here's the key to a very successful day: a very successful evening planning it. If you come to a big, busy day thinking you can just get ready for it in the morning, it's a recipe for disaster. You are going to feel stressed and overwhelmed before you've even started.

You have to reverse-engineer your success, and that is a key ingredient. Prepare the night before.

You want to spare your brainpower, which we don't have infinite amounts of. I like to think of brainpower like a cup of tea. Would you want to start the day with that cup already drained, and try to function for the rest of the day on an empty cup? If you plan the night before, when you come to your busy day, your cup is still full, and you can slowly drink it throughout the day.

Here's one example of how planning helps. You might have heard of very successful CEOs wearing the same outfit every day. Why? Because they're sparing their brainpower. They're not being lazy, they're being extremely efficient, because the less you have to think about in the morning, the more incredible your energy is going to be for the task at hand.

Eat the frog

Now, when it comes to the morning, you also have to have a ritual. Yes, I am talking about discipline, a word that we do not tend to like as adults. But today I want you to learn to not only like it, but fall in love with it. As children, we understandably associate discipline with punishment, and we can hold on to a resistance to it, but discipline is actually a superpower. In discipline, you'll find freedom, because you know how you need to act to get to a certain result. The secret to success is, in many aspects, about having a strong sense of self-discipline. And biohackers are extraordinary with their self-discipline.

So what does discipline look like in the morning? Well, you're going to have to 'eat the frog'. This concept comes from self-development expert Brian Tracy, who says if you 'eat a frog' first thing in the morning, everything else is going to feel easy in comparison. All this means is, you need to know your non-negotiable task for the day, the task that absolutely must be done – the one that we're often tempted to leave to the end of the day, but will hang over us and cause us anxiety if we do. You want to manage your time and bring that task to the top of your to-do list when your willpower cup is still full. Get it done, and then you can enjoy a calmer day.

When you are successful at getting your non-negotiable tasks done first thing, early in the day, you can then progressively move through the rest of your work with a sense of satisfaction and contentment, knowing that you've already eaten the frog. It's a brilliant way to manage stress because you're managing your time and productivity, and you have a roadmap for your working day.

3. The art of single gazing

The third hack is a visual one, backed up by neuroscience. I particularly love the work of neuroscientist Dr Andrew Huberman, who has done a fantastic job of explaining how visual acuity is directly connected to our ability to concentrate. Let me explain: imagine an eagle flying and scanning the horizon. It's a bit like a person who's not concentrating – looking left, right, up and down. Then suddenly, the eagle sees its prey. It locks on, the gaze is now really focused. This is called 'concentration arousal', and it is triggered when there is something we want to get. Just like eagles, we are hunters – despite evolution, the way we were built at a biological level is still the same now as it was a million years ago. You can use this tendency as a powerful tool to hack your concentration, and this is exactly how it works:

- With your eyes, lock on to a specific point not too far in front of you. It could be a button on your computer screen, or something that allows you to keep a straight gaze.
- Fixate on that point for one or two minutes.

This is not as easy as it sounds, and it will take a while to master. You might feel like you need to blink more, but actually it's worth trying to blink less and less. The sharper the image is, the more focused, the more concentrated you will become. It really is a pathway into concentration. What happens from a biohacking standpoint when you visually lock on to something is the release of two neurochemicals: epinephrine and acetylcholine. These are the neurotransmitters that help us concentrate. It's incredible that our sight is directly related to our ability to focus. Looking around is the enemy of concentration. Instead, you want to train yourself to lock on to something in your eyeline, find that solid gaze and then get into the piece of work you need to complete.

I learned this technique from a meditation teacher when I was living on a tiny island in Bali. The teacher said, 'If you want to master the art of meditation, you need to master the art of single gazing.' And he had a very specific meditation technique whereby we would sit down in a cross-legged position and look at the flame on a burning candle. It shows how yogic traditions, ancient traditions and neuroscience intertwine, and how whether you're looking at a computer button or a burning candle, the result is the same: heightened concentration, arousal of peak focus.

4. The biological rhythm

This one is all about how to take intelligent breaks. I used to have a lot of resistance to taking breaks, and what happened? I burned out.

Breaks are vital to your career success, and this is the one thing I wish I knew back when I was a lawyer.

What is a biological rhythm?

There are two types of biological rhythm, and they are hardwired into your DNA. You could think of them as your 'gene clocks'; they're part of your evolutionary blueprint. We can hack this part of your biology through tracking.

The first one is the circadian rhythm, which is often mentioned when people talk about sleep and is a cycle that repeats every twenty-four hours. But the one we're going to focus on is the ultradian rhythm, which repeats in much shorter bursts of around ninety minutes throughout the day. It's a bit like a roller coaster, going high and low from hour to hour, and it's written into our DNA as human beings.

So, this idea that you get out of the bed in the morning, go to work and then just keep going until you crash back into bed again, it's never going to work. Instead, you need to understand and work with your biological rhythms rather than against them.

What is an ultradian high?

An ultradian high is when you get to that peak performance state. You feel absolute sharpness, you're in the zone, your concentration is high, and nothing in this world can distract you. And then what happens? You dip into an ultradian low: you might get grumpy or hungry, you might start hankering for a coffee, maybe you get a bit fidgety or irritable. Often when we hit this low, we just try to push on. But trying to work harder when you've hit a dip in your biological cycle is a mistake. What you need to do instead is take a break.

This was a hard one for me to master, because I did not like the idea of taking any breaks at all – I'm pretty go, go, go. So how did

I personally approach this? By telling myself that breaks are 'intelligent' and that I deserve them. Once I'd convinced myself of this, then I allowed myself to take the breaks I needed – hopefully you can do the same.

What is an intelligent break?

There are two different styles of intelligent break that I want you to familiarise yourself with. The first one is very simple: talking a walk. But not just any walk: a walk where you're *not* going to listen to your favourite podcast or playlist. I know this can be a hard one, but we want to switch off to switch on. We want to rest to reset. If you read biographies, you might know that great minds like Charles Darwin, Ernest Hemingway, Albert Einstein and Sigmund Freud were all known for taking long, reflective walks. They all reported that when they came back, they had these ideas striking them like lightning. It's not a coincidence; during those walks, your brain gets a sort of massage. You switch off but you're allowing your brain to prepare for the next ultradian high, the next high on that roller coaster.

The second intelligent break I'd encourage you to incorporate into your days is yoga nidra or 'non-sleep deep rest' (see page 184). It's a technique I learned in an Indian ashram. You listen to someone reading a script that lasts twenty to thirty minutes, and during that time you close your eyes, breathe deeply and go inwards. This resets you; it is the healing response to the ultradian low. When you take an intelligent break like this, you can prepare yourself to ride the wave into peak performance once again. The reason I love this is because you can listen to a yoga nidra script anytime. Many people use this technique when they're sleep-deprived and they just need a quick twenty-minute rest. It's almost like a power nap for the brain, and is deeply relaxing. Think of your brain like an athlete; you'd never see an elite person skipping their recovery days, and your brain needs those moments of rest and release to return to peak performance.

Follow your bliss

The fifth and final biohack for your brain is one of my personal favourites: follow your bliss. Let's think about success for a moment. Success is a blueprint; there is a science to it, a certain roadmap you need to follow. But it is quite possible to be chasing success without ever taking a moment to ask yourself where your sense of enjoyment and fulfilment comes from. There was a time when I was in this position: I was very successful, as successful as I could be, but I hadn't sat down and asked myself if it was fulfilling me, if my career was giving me love and joy and contentment. For me, being of service and helping other people is crucial to fulfilment – it's the reason I wanted to be a lawyer in the first place – but then I burned out. That's when I realised I could help people – including myself – to thrive and still apply the same skill set but in a way that didn't risk my health.

This is the question I want to put to you: have you taken a moment to reflect and ask yourself, with absolute honesty, what makes you feel fulfilled? When you've had a very busy and stressful day and you go to bed at night, do you feel fulfilled? If not, why not? While success is a science, fulfilment is an art, because it's down to your individual personality. Fulfilment to you is probably different to what it looks like for others. Perhaps you have a specific passion or story – make that passion or that story your new portal into your sense of joy, accomplishment and bliss.

There's a quote from one of my favourite books, *Pathways to Bliss* by Joseph Campbell, that I hope inspires you to do exactly that. 'What is it we are questing for? Is it the fulfilment of that which is potential in each of us? Questing for it is not an ego trip. It is an adventure to bring into fulfilment your gift to the world, which is yourself.' And this is exactly it: you have that special gift or outlook that is unique to you, so bring it to the world. Let it blossom, let your personality shine and be sure of what it is you want to fulfil.

I believe that finding a sense of fulfilment is one of the best antidotes to burnout, because you can work for an extended amount of time, and you can work in a smart manner, but if you know that you are deeply fulfilled and content, you are a lot less likely to burn out.

When I spent time in the ashram, I was introduced to the concept of dharma. My yoga teacher taught me that the dharma is about finding your true calling, the thing that sets your soul on fire. In ancient Sanskrit it's dharma, in modern parlance you might call it 'the art of fulfilment', as coach Tony Robbins does. He says, 'The ultimate failure is to have a life filled with success without fulfilment.'

So here's my definition of bliss when it comes to your career: it is the sweet spot where passion, mission, sense of service to others, enjoyment and curiosity meet.

One of the fundamental ways to 'hack' into this bliss is to cultivate it. This is the challenge: whatever anxious thought you might be harbouring right now, let's try and transform it into a gratitude thought. For example, 'I'm so anxious about my presentation tomorrow because there are going to be so many people there,' could become, 'I am so deeply grateful that I get to present to such a big audience.' If the thought is 'I have to do this' try to reframe it to 'I get to do this'. Instead of feeling like something is happening *to* you, a mindset shift could mean you feel like it's happening *for* you and your eventual growth.

YOU

13. Breaking the comparison curse

Have you ever found yourself scrolling through Instagram after a bad day, feeling more and more resentful with every post you see that your life just doesn't live up to those of the people you follow? If so, you're not alone. Social media has been linked with increased rates of anxiety and depression, and research from the Royal Society of Public Health shows that much of this comes down to feelings of missing out and jealousy of friends and strangers who share their lives online. Having windows into the lives of thousands of people may make us feel more informed or connected, but it can also have a detrimental effect on our own self-esteem – and that is not our fault.

Comparison is an instinct that starts early. You only need to observe toddlers playing happily with red Lego until they see a peer playing with yellow and all hell breaks loose to know how ingrained it is. We compare lunchboxes at primary school, exam results and drinking stamina at university, and on it goes. This compulsive comparison can even be spotted in monkeys: a classic study by Frans de Waal at Emory University found monkeys were perfectly happy exchanging their stones for cucumber until other monkeys started getting grapes, at which point the cucumber monkeys went wild.

Various studies show how this tendency plays out throughout our lives. For example, it's rarely what we have that impacts our happiness, but what we have compared to others around us. Take a

2010 study by economist Angus Deaton and psychologist Daniel Kahneman, which found that it's how your income compares to that of your friends rather than how much you actually earn that affects your overall life satisfaction. The higher your income rank, the happier you feel. As our lives have increasingly moved online, seen through filtered windows and highlight reels, comparison culture has thrived. Photoshop was created thirty-six years ago, meaning we are the first generation to have grown up surrounded by images that are not real – pictures of blemish-free, trimmed-down perfection. Our formative years were dominated by TV shows and films that had yet to hear of diversity, broadcasting one incredibly narrow version of beauty, success, family and cultural norms. All this has understandably shaped the way we see ourselves, and the impossible and unrealistic standards to which we compare ourselves.

Back in 2019, *Stylist* conducted its own research that revealed the extent of the damage comparison culture was having on us. Though ninety-eight per cent of readers had a social media account, only one in twenty said they had high self-esteem. The biggest culprit in hindering a healthy sense of self? You guessed it: comparing our lives with those of others. When we delved further, asking readers what their real comparison trigger points were, it was 'people who make life look easy' that stung the most. The women who seemingly have it all together with barely a whiff of overwhelm, while we're all over the place. After that, forty-four per cent of our readers can't help but compare when they see others having amazing experiences, while seeing others' career success caused comparison in forty per cent. Thirty-eight per cent said that benchmarking where they're at in their life compared to their peers makes them feel inferior.

Overwhelmingly, it became clear that comparison has become a problematic lens through which we struggle to see ourselves and our successes clearly. It's something we must not be ashamed about — those numbers alone prove most of us are in the same boat, and science has shown it's human nature — but it is something we should be aware of and try to rein in so it doesn't impact our self-worth, motivation and appreciation for life.

So often, people throw out social media as the answer and the solution: simply stop using it, they say, and we'll feel better about ourselves. But in the modern world, it's not that simple, is it? It's inextricably linked with our lives in so many ways; some use it for work or to grow their business, some to find inspiration and ideas, some to socialise and meet new people. To simply suggest we unplug from the global network in order to stop comparing feels untenable and also plain unfair. Plus, there are plenty of ways to negatively compare ourselves to others that don't involve screens. To transform the way we view ourselves in relation to the people around us, we have to dig a little deeper.

How to use the PIP technique to overcome toxic comparison culture
by Lucy Sheridan

Lucy Sheridan is the world's first comparison coach and author of The Comparison Cure. *Here, she shares a technique that will help you to stop comparing yourself to others in a negative way and instead reap inspiration from them.*

What is the PIP technique?
'Finding your PIP, or "proof it's possible", is a method of dissolving comparison by stopping you from getting triggered by

certain people and learning to feel inspired by them,' Lucy explains. The PIP technique involves looking for people whom you admire who prove that it is possible to achieve your goals. 'They might be twenty years ahead of you, they might be one year ahead of you – it doesn't matter,' says Lucy, explaining that the key thing is that they have something that you would also like to have in the future.

'Comparison is based on myths, legends and lies. The PIP technique uses facts and data,' Lucy adds. She explains that it is based on a neuro-linguistic programming technique called modelling, which is a process of achieving the things you want by mastering the beliefs and thought processes that underlie other people's specific behaviours. 'PIP helps you to reprogramme your subconscious and stop comparison spirals. Your previous triggers can become inspiration,' Lucy says, adding, 'You can then apply that wisdom to yourself and turn it into action.'

How do you choose your PIP?

Lucy explains that it's a good idea to have multiple PIPs to avoid fixation on one person. You could have a PIP for different goals in your life, like money, family and work. 'Don't choose someone who is already a trigger for you when it comes to comparison,' Lucy says. Instead, look for new people who inspire you and who have taken the steps you need to take to get where you want to be.

Here are some questions you can ask yourself to figure out if a potential PIP is a good fit for you:

Are they someone you can study and find out more about?

'This might be a friend of a friend who you could go for a coffee with or someone you can speak to on the internet,' Lucy says. If you can establish where the contact might be, you can ensure that you can connect to them to help you learn more about them.

Do they represent what you truly want?

It's crucial to think about whether the thing that you're looking to this person for is something you are genuinely invested in. 'You may have inherited this desire from a family member, for example. Or maybe it was something you wanted five years ago and you haven't checked in with whether it is something you still want,' Lucy says.

Can you find at least one way in which you're similar to this person?

'Having a connective point to your PIP will stop you from putting that person on a pedestal,' Lucy says. The similarity might be something really simple, like the way you both speak or shared interests and hobbies, but it's important to identify this before choosing them as one of your PIPs.

Can you find at least three ways in which they inspire you?

The purpose of your PIP is to have a point of inspiration, so it's important to think about what it is that you find inspiring about this person and why that's relevant to you. 'Make sure they feel like someone who will fuel you to keep you going rather than making you feel lesser than,' Lucy says, explaining that it can be good to choose people who are open about how they got where they are.

How to use your PIP to help you focus on your goals

'Think about the things your PIP has done and which of those things you would and would not like to do,' Lucy advises. 'Maybe they have secured a certain job role that you want but they have had to move to Argentina for the job, which is not something you're interested in. Ask yourself, how can I get that same experience but find a different way to get there?'

Lucy explains that you can take clues from your PIP and the things they have done and find ways to apply these in your own life to help you realise what path you should follow, looking at things like their morning routines and life progression. You can write this information down in a journal and you can also have regular check-ins with your PIP to see if they are still relevant for you and your goals.

How to stop your PIP relationship from becoming toxic

'If you find yourself getting triggered by your PIP and you start comparing yourself to them in negative ways, they are probably not a good fit for you,' Lucy says. 'If this comparison does come up, ask yourself what's going on with you. You might not actually be jealous of the fact that they're on a beach in Italy with an Aperol, but resentful that you haven't made time for yourself to rest and meet your own needs.' Even if one PIP doesn't work out for this reason, it can still be a brilliant chance to reflect on yourself, which you can learn from.

Other techniques to try when you feel the creep of comparison

Tend to your triggers

First and most importantly, notice what situations or which people draw you into playing the comparison game. The sting of envy or inadequacy we feel when we compare ourselves to others is simply an alarm bell of dissatisfaction, and listening to it can help you figure out what you feel you're missing. For example, if the pang hits when you see someone posting about their idyllic holiday while you're sitting at your crumb-strewn keyboard on a Monday morning, it's not too much of a leap to understand why that's triggering and what you need – namely, a break. Perhaps it's a certain person whose humble-bragging about their achievements winds you up, or a work setting that always leaves you worrying you're not enough. Really stop and take stock in these moments where your inner critic rears up (especially if you were feeling fine ten minutes before) and consider what the trigger might have been. You'll get one step closer to figuring out how to nip it in the bud.

> **Journal prompt:** *Who or what frequently brings up feelings of jealousy and inadequacy for you? What is it about them, specifically, that makes you feel this way?*

Examine your self-talk

Self-talk is the inner voice that represents the way we feel about ourselves, and the beliefs and biases we have when it comes to who we think we are. It can have a huge impact on our emotions and behaviours. Healthy self-talk can be supportive and motivating, but negative self-talk can undermine our confidence. When we're comparing ourselves to others and coming up short, this is our inner critic at work. It might sound like, 'I'm not as good as them,' or 'I'd never be able to do that,' or 'There's no point trying to be better' – all examples of negative self-talk that can keep us stuck in a rut of despondency.

If thoughts like these come up when you're comparing yourself to others, try to challenge that inner critic. Stop and ask yourself if the thought is really true – is it rooted in evidence or is it exaggerated? It can help to put things into perspective, too. Say you're feeling bad about yourself after reading an article about a high-flying CEO who built a multimillion-pound company by the age of thirty. Interrupt your negative self-talk with some practical questions: What would you have had to miss out on or sacrifice in your life to have that same achievement to your name? How many people could realistically achieve this goal? When it came down to it, would you *really* want to be this person? Often, when we put things into real-world perspective, we can snap ourselves out of that oh-so-tempting spiral of self-criticism.

Journal prompt: *Think of a friend or loved one you admire. If they were comparing themselves negatively to others, what would you say to them?*

Don't knock the gratitude list

In those moments where you're feeling like life isn't fair (we all have them, because often it isn't) the word 'gratitude' can understandably make you want to roll your eyes. But there's a reason so many wellness gurus and spiritual guides see it as the starting point for true self-reflection, because there's power in focusing on what you do have instead of dwelling on what you don't. A leading gratitude researcher, Robert A. Emmons PhD, conducted multiple studies on the link between gratitude and wellbeing and found that feeling thankful effectively boosts mood and reduces the risk of depression. It can even impact your sleep, according to a 2011 study published in *Applied Psychology* that found writing in a gratitude journal for fifteen minutes before bed helped people sleep for longer and have a more restful night.

And when it comes to comparison, the benefits just keep racking up. Not only does gratitude boost your mood, which in turn makes you think more kindly about yourself, it can also reframe feelings of having it worse than others or not being good enough. Some people keep a gratitude journal, where they note down a handful of things they're grateful for every day – everything from the weather that allowed them to go for a walk before work to the funny message they received from a friend – but it's worth homing in on yourself when you're practising gratitude to tackle comparison. This shifts your view from everyone else to the most important person: you.

Journal prompt: If you don't know where to start, try writing for a couple of minutes on each of these prompts.

- *What compliments have you received that have stuck with you?*
- *What are three personality traits you're glad you have?*

- *What are three things you've been grateful for this week?*
- *What's one positive thing someone might notice about you when they meet you in a social setting?*
- *What's one positive thing someone might notice about you when they meet you in a work setting?*
- *What was an act of kindness that surprised you recently?*
- *What makes you feel lucky?*

Turn comparison into competition (with yourself)

Trying to live your life by other people's timelines or judging yourself against an external benchmark is often a recipe for disappointment. There are thousands of factors that feed into everyone's personal achievements, but often we only see the end result – that 'personal news' post announcing a big promotion or a new PB on Strava. This is why it tends to be much healthier and more motivating to compete against the only person who is in exactly the situation you are: yourself. If you're working on a weekend project, keep a note of how much you get done from one Sunday to the next; if you're trying to get stronger, keep track of how much weight you can lift every session. Set small, achievable goals and watch yourself smash through them. Soon, other people's journeys will become pleasant background noise.

Journal prompt: *What's one thing you'd like to get better at? How can you set some time aside for it in your week and track your progress?*

Make social media work for you

While the online world and the way we use it to interact with others is deeply ingrained in our lives now, it can be empowering to remember that we have control over what we engage with, and when. Whether you spend most of your screen time on Instagram, X or TikTok, take ten minutes to intentionally scroll through your feed and really notice who or what makes you feel engaged or inspired, versus the content that makes you feel unsettled or unhappy. It's easy to mindlessly consume huge amounts of information in a short space of time without really realising the impact it's having on us, but by curating our feeds around what feels good, we can limit that post-scroll sadness. If someone or something is making you feel bad about yourself or your life, unfollow or mute them – your feeds are for you and you alone.

Limiting the time you spend taking in information about other people's lives is important too – we're talking anything from LinkedIn to global news – because everything about the internet is designed to keep us using it indefinitely. A 2023 study from Swansea University found that people who reduced their social media usage by fifteen minutes a day over a period of three months significantly improved their mental and physical health: they were less likely to get colds, saw a thirty per cent reduction in depressive symptoms and experienced a fifty per cent jump in sleep quality. It's not about seeing social media as something inherently toxic or bad for us, but rather making sure we use it on our own terms. Take control of your screen time. Use your phone settings to set limits for the apps you use most (i.e. thirty minutes a day on Instagram), after which you'll get a notification telling you to wrap it up. Try putting your phone 'to sleep' after a certain time in the evening, and avoid picking it up as a distraction technique when you're working – walk around and stretch instead to get the blood flowing and re-energise yourself.

Journal prompt: *How much time, ideally, would you spend looking at your phone each day? What do you want to get out of that time, e.g. laughter, social connection, awareness of what's happening in the world, fun? How can you be more intentional about using your phone for this specific purpose?*

14. How to be more confident in the ways that matter

Confidence feels amorphous. We most often think of it in relation to how someone looks: do they walk with their chin up and their shoulders back? Do they dress and present themselves in a way that says 'I want you to see me' or do they shrink and hide in every sense of the word? While this is *one* way we signify confidence, it's a small and frankly superficial part of the puzzle. We all know people who appear, outwardly, to be the life and soul of any party or the biggest presence in any room, yet harbour a great deal of insecurity in who they are and what they have to offer in the world. True confidence comes from a much deeper place: a sense of self-worth.

It's no secret that in many ways, women in particular are admonished for appearing 'too' confident. We qualify our thoughts with 'maybe' and 'I just wondered'; we apologise even when we're not in the wrong; we make ourselves smaller so we don't ruffle feathers or come across as full of ourselves. But what does it mean to be full of yourself, really? That you are your number-one cheerleader? That you believe in your own convictions, and your right to contribute them? That you don't constantly second-guess and stifle yourself in favour of making others more comfortable? That you are the *fullest* version of yourself?

The fear of being labelled any one of the negative words thrown out to keep confident women down ('bossy', 'arrogant', 'vain', to name a few) has held too many of us back from showing up as the brilliant, opinionated, powerful people we all have the potential to be. Working on your confidence is a crucial part of telling not only the world, but yourself, that you deserve to take up space in it.

There are three key strands to building true confidence, which we'll explore here: breaking down unhelpful beliefs about yourself, trusting your own convictions and finding (and using) your authentic voice.

 ### The confidence masterclass: How to believe that you can, and you will

by Hattie MacAndrews

Hattie MacAndrews founded five companies before she turned thirty and is now a qualified confidence coach with a practical and curious approach to helping women step into self-belief and stem self-doubt.

'Being an entrepreneur at the age of nineteen, I naturally faced imposter syndrome and a lack of confidence, which I had to get over if I was going to be successful. That experience has meant I wanted to become a coach to others, particularly women, who had that voice in their head telling them they weren't good enough. That's where loads of barriers stem from, in the women I coach: I'm not funny enough, I'm not pretty enough, I'm not clever enough. Fundamentally, that's what a lack of confidence is: the belief that you're not enough in some way, and that is a very limiting belief.

'It can come from stories we tell ourselves; it can come from experiences we have in the workplace, or experiences we have at home or in our relationships, and we can build this negative narrative about ourselves throughout our lives that chips away at us until we're left with no confidence. Once you've got to that point, it's very difficult to work out how to build your confidence and how to get back that self-assurance we all have in childhood but that is often taken away from you.'

Why is it important to have confidence?

'When you feel confident, you can back yourself. You believe in yourself, and that's when your world really opens up and you don't feel limited.

'For some people, that might mean believing they can work their way up to CEO of their company, while for others it might be believing that they will be a brilliant partner or parent – we all have different goals, but that feeling of self-belief is what propels all of us towards them.

'Once you have that confidence, you don't need to seek validation from elsewhere, you don't need to be always searching for external proof that you are good enough. Once you inherently feel it, you believe that you are capable of something, and that alone means you're far more likely to achieve it. It just opens doors in so many aspects of life, and if you really invest in building your confidence, there's not much that can hold you back.'

What is the most common misconception about confidence?

'A lot of people think they're either innately confident or they're not. They'll say, "This is just the kind of person I am. I'm never going to be confident enough to perform in front of people, or ask that person to mentor me, or go on holiday by myself" –

whatever it may be. But holding on to that belief means you're static, you're never going to move towards the thing you want to do because you've told yourself you never will, and so it becomes a self-fulfilling prophecy.

'Confidence is so far from being that black and white; in fact, some people might feel really confident at work and in their career potential, but then not feel confident at all when they go on dates or are in social spaces, for example. And that is OK, that's totally normal. Self-belief can ebb and flow in various aspects of our life and throughout our lives. Some days you might wake up and feel really empowered and strong; some days you might think, "I just don't have it in me to do this". But that underlying foundation of self-belief is something everyone can build, and it's like forming a new habit. You have to practise it. You have to set yourself goals and check in and be consistent to get there.'

So where do I start?

'When I'm working with someone on confidence, it always pays to start small. That first goal might seem, to someone else, like the smallest, most inconsequential thing, but it's vital in getting the ball rolling and starting to break down that "not enough" belief. For instance, I had a client who didn't want to go out in public unless she was extremely well-groomed and put together, and we worked out that it all came down to a lack of confidence. She wanted to be able to go out with no make-up on, with her hair not perfectly done, but it felt like a huge leap. So the first thing she did was just go to the pub with friends with her hair in a bun – which may seem like nothing to most people, but it was a big deal to her. And she had a

wonderful night and realised that barely anyone noticed, no
one made any assumptions about what that said about her, the
world didn't crumble. Sometimes it takes a small thing to start
chipping away at that self-judgement and building up your own
evidence that you are deserving of showing up in the world
however you want to.

'Identify one area of your life where you want to feel more
confident, whether that be at work, in your social life, or
something else. Then try and understand why your confidence is
lacking there: were you brought up in a household where you
were doubted or criticised? Were you belittled by a former boss?
Have you been left out by a group of friends who weren't inviting
you to lunch? Try to pinpoint where your belief that you're not
enough might have come from, or what has reinforced it. Once
you recognise that, it can be much easier to dismantle the truth of
it and let it go: my family had different values to me so that's why
they criticised me; my boss was going through intense stress at
that time and took it out on me; my friends probably just assume
I'm always busy, there's no real evidence they don't want to be
friends with me.

'Then set yourself small, sustainable goals to build up your
confidence. What's the one thing you can do that week to help
yourself feel a little more confident? It might be inviting a
colleague you haven't spoken to before to grab lunch, or
going for a twenty-minute drink by yourself without using your
phone or a book as armour, or watching a quick YouTube
video of how to use some of the machines at the gym so you
feel a bit more prepared to go there alone. Something that will
give you a sense of reward, of getting out of your comfort
zone so you can feel proud of yourself. That feeling of pride is

so powerful because it retrains those neural pathways that keep telling you you can't. You've started proving to yourself that you can, and you will.'

Why you should be feedback fasting

How many times do you ask someone else for advice each day? Not just crucial, life-changing advice that often requires the help of your loved ones, but small things, like which dress you should wear to a party or how you should phrase an email to your boss. The reality is that we're probably all asking other people for advice way more than we realise.

This isn't necessarily a bad thing. Research shows that the 'wisdom of crowds' can benefit decision-making. But asking other people for advice all the time can impact your ability to make your own choices, which could affect your self-confidence. 'Our wants are completely unique to us and listening to our whole intelligence and paying attention to the nudges we feel is so important,' says Lucy Sheridan, the comparison coach we met in Breaking the Comparison Curse (see page 213). 'We often override our instincts by asking for advice.'

This doesn't mean you should never ask for advice again. Instead, Lucy recommends a practice called a feedback fast, where you don't ask for advice from anyone for a week. 'Don't put your outfit choice in a WhatsApp group, don't ask your friends for their opinion on someone you're dating, don't run ideas past your boss if you don't need to,' Lucy says, explaining how the feedback fast works. 'Acting based on your own autonomy is actually really radical, and [even] independent, confident people will be shocked at how much reassurance they might seek,' Lucy adds.

Whether you feel terrified by the idea of making decisions on your own or you simply want to save some time by preventing conversations about which shade of white you should buy a top in, these are Lucy's tips for doing your own feedback fast.

How to make decisions for yourself during your feedback fast

Just because you have stopped asking people for advice, it doesn't mean you're immediately going to feel confident in your own decisions. If you are feeling unsure, Lucy recommends using a journal to write down your thoughts and ideas on a subject until you feel more confident in the decision you are making.

'You can also plan a daily self-care check-in, maybe after you brush your teeth, and look at the ways you advocated for yourself that day, [then] use the information you learned to understand how you can become a better decision-maker,' Lucy says.

What to take away from a feedback fast

Lucy explains that the feedback fast should act as a reset, so you can figure out how much you trust yourself and what you can do to improve that. Some of the things you should take into account are:

- In which areas of your life do you not trust yourself? For example, are you always asking people what to do at work, even though you're fully capable of doing your job to a high standard?
- Who are you asking for advice from? Lucy explains: 'Just because people have strong opinions, it doesn't mean they're always well-placed [to advise you].' Asking your mum about dating, for example, when she has been married for thirty years and is bewildered by dating apps, might be frustrating and unproductive.

When you've identified the areas and the people you're struggling with, you can make a plan for how to improve them. Figure out how you can learn to have more confidence in specific areas of your life and who the best people are to turn to if you do need help with something specific.

How to start asking for advice again after your feedback fast

After your feedback fast is over, you can begin to ask advice of others again. But be conscious about how often you are doing so and the ways in which you are asking people for help. 'Rather than laying out all of the information to people and asking for permission, figure out where you stand on the subject first and present that viewpoint to them,' Lucy suggests. 'Share updates with people instead of requesting opinions.'

This will probably mean that you wait longer before you share something with someone, which will help you become clearer and more decisive in your decisions. 'It isn't about keeping secrets from your friends,' Lucy says. 'It's just repositioning how you share what's going on in your life – it means your friends can be your friends again rather than a panel of experts.'

 How to speak so people listen
by Samara Bay

Samara Bay has been a Hollywood dialect coach for more than a decade, working with world-famous actors on some of the biggest blockbusters, from Wonder Woman to Guardians of the Galaxy. But it was when she turned her hand to coaching women who were running for political office that she realised how much voice, confidence and the way we view power are intertwined.

What are the most common misconceptions about public speaking?

'The general consensus is that in order to seem confident when speaking in public, and in order to be taken seriously, we must try to sound like the straightest, whitest, richest man we know. We've all been taught that this is the archetype of power and authority. But unless that is actually who you are, you'll always be left chasing something you're not.

'It's worth pausing at this point and thinking, "Wait, I don't want to live in a future that looks like the past. I actually have an opportunity and responsibility to start shifting that archetype of authority in people's minds, instead of trying to force myself into that one-dimensional mould." That old standard may have served a purpose once, but we have outgrown it as a society. There are so many more of us who are worthy of being heard.

'The first step is to try to think of people you admire who are using their voices in a way that feels fresh and isn't a symbol of the old framework of power. Some people say to me, "Actually, my grandmother is strong in a surprising way and she knows how to use her voice without changing it." A lot of people in the United States turn to politician and activist Alexandria Ocasio-Cortez; she is proof that you can sound like where you're from, that you don't have to spend the majority of your time in public trying to dial down or hide who you are. Because the energy it takes to hide and shapeshift is so vast.

'The other misconception is that public speaking is fundamentally fear-based and not fun. Yes, our nervous systems can be triggered at first; our earliest ancestors were survivalists, and when they saw eyes on them, that signalled a predator and mortal danger. But through my own experience of coaching thousands of people, largely women, I've realised there is something else at play that goes beyond the physiological reaction.

'The fact is, unless we fit the traditional, age-old portrait of power and authority – which women do not – we are projecting our voices into an environment that was not built for us, that doesn't respect the way we sound, the pitch of our voices, the language we use quite as much. So we have that to contend with too.'

Why is it so important to be a confident speaker?
'Firstly, for many of us our jobs require us to represent ourselves
well verbally, whether that be a pitch, a presentation, a private
conversation about a promotion or talking to camera for an
Instagram reel. That is just the world we live in now.

   'More important than the practical side, though, is the way
we think about our voices, and our public-speaking ability is a
stand-in for how seriously we take ourselves. It's about self-
worth. Allowing our ideas that live on the inside to come out,
the very essence of speaking, requires a huge amount of bravery
and self-trust – which is the very definition of confidence. So at
the heart of it all, it's about whether you believe you deserve to
take up time and space. Speaking publicly shows yourself that
you do, so it's a self-fulfilling act of confidence.'

**Where do I start in becoming a more confident
speaker?**
'The first thing is to know that more people feel discomfort
about the way they sound than don't. You are not alone in that,
and as I touched on earlier, there is nothing fundamentally
wrong with the way you talk, no matter what you've been told
before.

   'I've worked with female politicians who've come to me with a
list of vocal tics and habits they've been told they need to fix –
perhaps they use filler words such as "like" or "um", or they
speak quite fast, or they've been told they should speak in a
lower register. But the truth is once you start to think a little
deeper about why the voices of women and people from
marginalised groups are seen as less authoritative or less
professional, you start to realise that those things are surface

level, that they all stem from trying to take up less space.
Working on the belief that you have a right to speak, that is what
will make you the best speaker.

'What I mean by that is, being yourself is powerful. When
you're speaking in public, your instinct might be to dial down
your accent, to filter out any idiosyncratic language – to come
across as generic as possible, essentially. So you're putting all
your energy into changing your voice, rather than connecting
and speaking with passion. But consciously and subconsciously,
people pick up on that. They see you're not passionate about
the topic and they wonder why *they* should be passionate about
the topic. They may struggle to find you convincing –
trustworthy, even.

'We have a lifetime of practice in speaking like we don't really
care about the things [we actually care a lot about]. It's a
defence mechanism: "Oh, I was thinking about having this party,
but no pressure if you don't feel like coming", "Oh, I had this
idea, but I'm not wedded to it, just throwing it out there". It's an
attempt to protect ourselves, but it actually has the opposite
effect of the one we want, where we're almost talking people out
of getting on board.

'Speaking with passion, conviction and authenticity is the key
to speaking well. Every viral political speech, every major TED
Talk, has connected because it is clear how much the person
cares. It is clear they are talking as themselves, not as anybody
else. Vulnerability is strength.'

What to do when negative thoughts knock your confidence

We all know holding on to negative beliefs about ourselves is extremely unhelpful and can be a serious confidence knock, but it can be difficult to let go of pessimistic thoughts, particularly if they're long-standing. Not only can thinking about yourself in a bad light lead to overthinking and self-deprecation, but it can also hold you back from achieving your goals. Gemma Perlin, a behavioural change coach specialising in neuro-linguistic programming, says it's very common to have limiting beliefs about yourself, even if you're not aware of them.

'A limiting belief is anything that holds you back from achieving what you want,' says Perlin, adding that tackling them head-on can be the easiest way to deal with them. To do this, she's developed a three-step technique that will help you stop overthinking and start achieving your goals.

Step 1: Awareness

Limiting beliefs may be common, but that doesn't mean that they're easy to identify right away. 'Often we feed ourselves negativity without even realising we're doing it,' Perlin says. Therefore, the first step to dealing with limiting beliefs is recognising them — for example, are you prone to thinking you won't be able to finish a workout, or have a good conversation with a friend, or complete a piece of work to your boss's satisfaction? 'Every time you notice yourself saying you can't do something or you shouldn't do something, take note of what it is you're actually saying about yourself,' says Perlin. You might think these things, say them out loud or even write them down. 'Journaling can be helpful, so you can look back on what you've written and identify any limiting beliefs.'

Step 2: Solutions

Once you have identified what your limiting beliefs are, you can plan how you want to deal with them – often the hard evidence is right in front of you that they're simply not rooted in fact. 'Do think about what support you need and whether or not you're surrounded by the right kind of people,' Perlin says. If you think certain people in your life are encouraging your negative thoughts about yourself, a good first step is to speak to them about why. Or maybe you might need to make a lifestyle change to help you deal with a limiting belief, particularly if you notice your negative thoughts arising at particular times, like when you're hung-over, for example.

Step 3: Acceptance

Dealing with limiting beliefs in the long term means truly accepting that they aren't true, according to Perlin. 'Solutions are important in the short term, but you need to truly accept that those ideas you have about yourself aren't accurate in order to move on from them.' Do this by replacing your current negative perceptions of yourself with new, positive beliefs. 'Figure out how you can turn negative voices down, or at least move them to the other shoulder, so you can welcome in positive, productive beliefs,' Perlin says. Focus on the things you have proven you can do, and try to hold those in your mind every time a negative thought occurs. Over time, your mind will reach for your strengths rather than those inaccurate limiting beliefs.

Prone to overthinking? Here's how to trust your gut

Self-doubt is seriously difficult to deal with. Not only can it lower your self-esteem, but it might also affect your ability to make decisions. You've probably experienced gut feelings before, but how many times have you listened to them? There are very few people who can say that they regularly make decisions based on their intuition, even though doing so can be beneficial to us in so many ways. It's a concept lots of us aren't sure we really believe in – but believing in your own bone-deep knowledge can be powerful.

Intuition is the idea that individuals can make successful choices without deliberate, analytical thought. It sounds nice, right? Overthinking has become second nature for so many of us. Because of that, the idea that you can have confidence in all your decisions because of an unconscious feeling might seem hard to grasp.

But actually, there are many ways to get in touch with your intuition. In fact, research shows that women have a greater ability to do so than men. Women's corpus callosum – the tissue that connects the two sides of the brain – is thicker than men's, which means that the logical and intuitive parts of our brains are more interconnected. Scientists have suggested that this may mean women are more inclined to combine logic and intuition when solving a problem, joining the dots between what we know and what we feel.

There are a variety of things that might be preventing you from accessing and acting on your gut feelings, however. This is what psychotherapist Lizandra Leigertwood helps her clients explore. 'I help people to deal with anxiety and calm the nervous system so they're not reacting from a place of stress and trauma,' she says.

'People have a very difficult time trying to work out the difference between anxiety and intuition, because both of those things take place within the stomach,' Leigertwood continues, explaining that the inability to differentiate between these two feelings is often a result of past trauma. 'Learning to get in touch with your intuition is a process of learning to trust yourself – often you might be doubting your feelings,' she says. Here, Leigertwood shares her tips for how you can improve your intuition by dealing with issues like anxiety, self-doubt and people-pleasing.

Check in with how you feel each day

If you're unable to access your intuition, it might be because you don't understand the feelings you're having and why you're having them. Leigertwood therefore recommends that you interrogate your feelings and work out if you're reacting to situations from a place of anxiety.

'Recognise what the beliefs are behind the way you're reacting and if there is any fear behind your decisions,' she advises. 'There's a real difference between fear and intuition, and the more that you build up your self-awareness, the more you'll be able to differentiate between the two.'

Journal regularly using the 'thought diary' technique

A great way to keep track of how you're feeling is to journal regularly. Leigertwood recommends trying out a thought diary. 'With a thought diary, you focus on writing about your feelings and your behaviours and find the connection between the two,' she explains. 'Write down your thoughts to figure out what is a rational thought and what is an irrational thought. Ask yourself, are you basing that feeling on fact or on assumption?'

Figure out what you like and what you don't like

As well as being in touch with your emotions, it's crucial to have good self-awareness if you're looking to get more in touch with your intuition. 'Pay attention to what makes you feel uncomfortable, as well as acknowledging the things that make you feel safe,' Leigertwood says. 'When you know what makes you feel safe, you'll be more aware of the things that make you feel unregulated.' Thinking about this consciously will improve your ability to make unconscious decisions because you'll be more naturally in touch with your preferences.

Let go of the fear of making mistakes

The reason so many people are prone to overthinking is the fear of getting something wrong. But Leigertwood says that it's really important to let go of this fear. 'We want to have that certainty that if we make the decision, it's going to be the right one, but sometimes making a quick decision is more useful for you and those around you than making what you might consider to be the right decision,' she explains.

Leigertwood suggests that you experiment with making impulse decisions about small things in your life, such as what travel route you're going to take or what you're going to have for lunch. When you see that these decisions mostly turn out OK, you'll have more confidence in making bigger decisions based on your instincts. 'This will help you learn to trust that your first judgement is usually the right one, rather than second-guessing yourself,' Leigertwood advises.

Avoid thinking about other people's responses

If you're prone to people-pleasing, you might be making decisions based on how other people will respond, as opposed to what you really want. 'Intuition is an unconscious knowing, but we've been conditioned to ignore it,' Leigertwood says. 'Your initial reaction is usually based on what you want, so that is the best option to go with.' Just like with overthinking, the best way to get over people-pleasing in this case is to experiment following your instinct based on what you want and looking at how people react to that. As long as you have good intentions, their reactions probably won't be as bad as you think.

Always prioritise self-care

You're more likely to be able to access and respond to your gut feelings when you feel happy and comfortable in yourself. Looking after yourself is the best way to reach this point. 'Make sure that you're spending time doing the things you enjoy and making time for rest,' Leigertwood says. 'When you pay attention to what your needs are and meet those needs, you're more likely to feel aligned with yourself.'

Five quickfire confidence hacks

1. Keep a compliment journal

It's human nature that we can receive scores of compliments in a day and yet the one piece of criticism is the thing that sticks. Try to get out of the habit and focus on the compliments you receive by keeping a note of them. It's not big-headed or vain – these are views other people actually hold about you, so much so that they've voiced them out loud, and it's worth reminding yourself of them.

2. Reflect on your positive traits

This is more about what you respect and admire about yourself, and yes, it may feel uncomfortable at first. But try to make a list on paper or in your phone's Notes app of things you like about yourself. Are you creative? Are you a great problem-solver? Are you fun? Are you a positive thinker? Write down at least seven positive attributes and keep them for reference whenever you're feeling unsure of yourself.

3. Celebrate your successes

In a society where humility is heralded, we can think it distasteful to shout about how wonderful we are, but it's very important to properly acknowledge when we've done something well. Whether it's a promotion, a winning goal in a football match or making a good new friend, celebrate the positive things in your life in big and small ways. Give yourself a treat or have a gathering of loved ones, and glow with pride unashamedly.

4. Have a confidence role model

We all come across people in life whom we admire for the way they put themselves out there and ooze self-belief. If they're not in your orbit – a celebrity, for example – try to mindfully pinpoint what it is that they do that makes them seem confident, and think about how you might emulate that. If they are someone you know, ask them to discuss it; chances are they'll be flattered and willing to give you their insight.

5. Try something brand new

It sounds simple, but doing something new, from cooking a new recipe to trying a new workout class to taking up an instrument, can be a powerful way to prove to yourself that you're capable of more than you expect. Even if the outcome isn't perfect (it rarely will be) the act alone of betting on yourself and broadening your horizons is a major confidence boost.

15. How to thrive alone

by Francesca Specter

Francesca Specter is a writer, podcaster and the author of
Alonement: How To Be Alone and Absolutely Own It. *She's been*
advocating for the importance of alone time since 2018, and has
done extensive research into why it's so vital for our psychological,
emotional and physical health. Here, she tells us how it's done right.

This is where you get to satisfy your curiosity over what makes
solitude into a positive, fulfilling experience, a concept I call
'alonement'. This is such a relevant and useful topic after the
pandemic, when we all had either far too much alone time or far too
little of it. Either we were spending our time working from home, away
from our colleagues, and perhaps even living alone during lockdown,
or we had too much time cooped up with our partner or housemates,
and now we just need a little bit of time to ourselves, but we're not
necessarily used to having it. Alonement has huge benefits universally
for personal growth and for learning who you are and what you like
as a person. The capacity to be comfortably alone is crucial to living
your fullest, most satisfying life.

<u>What is alonement?</u>

Why am I so passionate about this subject, you might wonder? Well, the answer is not that I've always naturally been someone who pursues alone time, in fact, up until 2018, alone time was my biggest fear. I was always a very gregarious extrovert who avoided alone time at all costs, and I just put that down to my personality. However, in 2018 things changed: I went through a break-up of a long-term relationship and I found myself single and living alone for the first time in my life. During that time, I realised that there were actually consequences to my fear of being alone. I'd book out my calendar with plans that I didn't even want to do, just to avoid my own thoughts. I would make absolutely no time for self-care, and I'd go on some god-awful, terrible dates just to avoid my own company. Eventually, I decided that enough was enough: I needed to stop acting out of fear of my own company and confront the thing I was so scared of.

In January 2019, I made a new year's resolution: to learn to be alone, and like it. In order to do this, I did two things. Firstly, I coined a word – alonement – to describe the experience of having alone time in a positive, meaningful way. Secondly, I built up my alone time incrementally. It started with leaving one night on the weekend free for me to spend a bit of time doing self-care or watching a movie alone and getting more comfortable with that. Eventually, I started challenging myself, so I'd go out for brunch by myself on a Saturday, something I'd never done before. And then I was doing bigger, more exciting, more daring things, like going to the cinema alone, taking myself out for three-course meals, and even going on solo trips to Berlin and Paris.

What I realised was, far from just being a Plan B to avoid my fear of being alone, this journey that I was on was changing my life for the better in so many ways. I was calmer, I was more confident, and I had a better sense of who I was and what mattered to me and what my values were. I also became more curious about the world around me, because suddenly my interests mattered. I wasn't just dictating my life around who would hang out with me at the weekend or what someone else wanted to do.

I've since learned that all the benefits of alone time I was experiencing were no coincidence. Psychologist Virginia Thomas released a study in 2019 where she spoke about the benefits that being alone had for a group of teenagers she'd been researching. Rather than being 'loners' or feeling lonely, those who chose alone time actively developed a better capacity for positive self-acceptance.

Solitude skills

Growing up as an extrovert, I used to think that solitude was something that either you were good at or you were bad at. But what I learned from Virginia Thomas's research is that being alone is a skill that you can develop and practise over time. The emotional toolkit that you need for this is made up of what she calls solitude skills. There are five vital solitude skills that helped me learn to love alone time: sitting with your own thoughts; planning your alone time and making it into quality time; spending time alone in public places; learning to communicate your alone time needs to the people in your life who you care about; and learning to balance your solitude with your social time.

Solitude skill 1: Sitting with your thoughts

The first solitude skill is learning to sit with your own thoughts. Now, this is the tough one – I know that I used to struggle with it, and occasionally I still do. It is one of those things that puts so many of us off spending time alone because we have to sit there and confront whatever's bothering us. There's no getting around it: this is uncomfortable. And the bad news is that sitting with your own thoughts is kind of necessary for learning to be comfortably alone. When I had the philosopher Alain de Botton on my podcast, he spoke about how you can be physically alone, but if you're not confronting your own thoughts – if you're, say, scrolling your phone or obsessively checking the news or something like that – then you're not really alone with yourself. So, yes, this is kind of a non-negotiable entrance fee into alonement. The good news is, there are so many techniques that can help us become comfortable with our own thoughts, and often they're things that you will probably have tried already, like meditation (see page 203), journaling (see below) or breathing exercises (see page 193). Even integrating just five minutes or so of these practices into your day can help you to learn to be more comfortable being with yourself. So I'm going to run through two exercises that are really handy for this purpose.

Exercise 1: Guided journaling

Try this three-minute guided journaling session. This one is going to be based on three simple writing prompts, spend one minute on each.

- *How are you feeling today?* Take a minute to write and reflect.
- *What's setting you back today?* Write down those thoughts.
- *What is energising you today?* See what comes to mind.

Journaling is a really good way of integrating a little bit of alonement into your everyday life and bringing that sense of intention and mindfulness to your every day. Ultimately, it helps you realise that confronting your thoughts isn't all that scary; it can just be done in three minutes on a piece of paper.

Exercise 2: Body scan

The next technique I'd like you to practice is a body scan, which we also covered in our chapter on rest, and for anyone who's ever tried the Headspace app or the Calm app, or really any kind of guided meditation, you may well be familiar with this. It's simply bringing attention to each part of the body in order to create a sense of awareness and comfort, sitting with yourself in your own skin. Use the script below to record your own guided meditation (or ask a friend with a particularly soothing voice) so that you can come back to it anytime you need it. For this two-minute exercise, make sure you're sitting comfortably in a chair with your feet planted on the ground, ready to begin. Close your eyes and follow your recorded instructions.

Start by taking deep breaths in: four, three, two, one. And deep breaths out: four, three, two, one. Keep that deep inhale, exhale going, and we're going to start by scanning down the body.

Begin from your head, noticing how you're feeling. Tune in to your forehead, your eyelids, your jaw. Notice any tension or discomfort in those areas. And remember you are just noticing it, you're not trying to cure anything or relax anything; it's just acknowledging what's going on there.

*Now you're moving down your neck into your shoulders and
your chest, and you're still breathing in and out of that space
slowly. If you can feel any tightness, any tension, again just bring
awareness to that, don't try and overanalyse it.*

*We're moving on down your arms, down your biceps, down
the elbows, forearms, fingers, noticing any stiffness. Next, pan
down through your stomach and move into your pelvis, your
legs. Noticing your weight in the chair. And finally moving down
to your feet. Feeling your toes and the sensation of the soles of
your feet on the floor.*

The idea of these exercises is to help us understand that spending time
alone doesn't need to be as hard as we make out when we're
imagining it. Simple two- or three-minute techniques, practised on a
daily basis, can really help to get you in tune with yourself and make
the inside of your head frankly a much less scary space.

Solitude skill 2: Planning time alone
This is all about putting a framework around your alone time and
making it into quality, enjoyable and fulfilling time.

Exercise 1: Make a list of things you enjoy
To get the ball rolling, start with a writing exercise. Make a list of the
activities that make you feel like *you*. For example, mine would be
going for a run on London's Hampstead Heath, making a really
delicious spaghetti bolognese, or just sitting at home and watching
back-to-back episodes of the US edition of *The Office*. Set a timer and
think about what activities matter to you.

Exercise 2: Being alone intentionally – going on a solo date

The best way to explain a solo date is planning something really special for yourself as you might do for a date night with a partner or a special occasion with a friend. This might seem silly, and you might think, 'Oh, my alone time just comes in the gaps between social plans,' but you need to remember that a plan with yourself is a valid plan. And that's the whole basis of solo dates. So the first thing you need to do when you're planning your solo date is simply to schedule it. Set a date and a time and stick to it. This allows you to look forward to the time and plan nice things that you might do during it.

Positive selfishness: When you're thinking up your solo date, be very specific. It isn't just about setting one activity to last you the whole afternoon or evening that you've set aside for yourself. It's also thinking, what food might you like to cook? Or what music might you like to be listening to? Or what kind of candle might you want to light? Again, this might sound silly if you're not used to doing it for yourself, but think about it: if you were planning a hot date night, you would consider all of these things. Give yourself the same courtesy. This is a really good time to practise what I call *positive selfishness*. This means thinking intensely of yourself in a way that doesn't affect anyone else, and often it can be doing those things that you don't get to do with other people. Say your partner really doesn't like eating spicy food, take that night by yourself to cook a whole Mexican feast just for you. When we get to fulfil these desires in our solitude, it means we don't resent or blame other people for not wanting to do these things.

Switching off: The next hugely important tip is to switch off your phone. We know now that we can get so distracted by our phones that we aren't actually with ourselves. In your alone time, when you've designated a whole evening to be by yourself, it's particularly important that you don't get distracted by someone else's WhatsApp drama or whoever is going out on Instagram, because that will only give you FOMO, and this is a date with you.

Getting ready: This might be as simple as putting on a freshly cleaned pair of your favourite pyjamas, or you might decide to put on a dress and lipstick if that makes you feel good. All these tips are basically centred around respecting and valuing this time that you're spending with yourself as you might do with another person. It reinforces over time that you matter, and you are worth doing these things for.

Solitude skill 3: Being alone in public

Being alone isn't just about sitting at home; it can also be a skill that you develop to occupy public spaces when you're flying solo. Now, if going to a restaurant or the cinema by yourself doesn't come naturally to you, then don't worry. It's not you, it is normal.

The basic infrastructure of our society is all based around being in groups of two or more. Think about how the tables are set up when you walk into a restaurant or a café; OK, there are a few places with counter dining, but generally it does look like the world is built for twos. The other thing that might put you off being alone in public is marketing. When you see an advertisement for a theme park, for instance, it usually shows a group of people. Or you might see an offer for two-for-one theatre tickets, and it makes you feel like you need to take someone else to watch a movie or a show in a darkened room. All this feeds into our sense that we can't be alone in public. But the good news is, we can.

If you fear judgement about it or you're worried that you're going to look like a loner or like you have no friends, rest assured that these fears are normal, but also kind of wrong. There is something called the 'spotlight effect', a phenomenon whereby we hugely overestimate the amount that others are looking at us and noticing us when we're doing something unusual like being alone in public. This is an example of a cognitive bias created by the fact that we are naturally egocentric (our worlds revolve around us) and often believe that our thoughts about ourselves are shared by the people around us.

Armed with that knowledge, imagine you didn't have any fear around being judged or seen by other people, that they weren't looking at you or thinking about you at all, really. Think about it; the world is your solo oyster. Make a list of things you'd like to do alone in public.

When you've got your list, the question is, how are you going to get around to doing all of this when you're not used to it? There are a few techniques that I started practising when I first explored the world of public alonement.

Technique 1: Exposure therapy

First, I decided I was going to take myself out for coffee. As simple as that sounds, I had never really thought to do it before. I took a book, sat in a coffee shop and realised that the world didn't end and pretty much no one was looking at me. I built up from there to things like going to the cinema by myself; I decided one weekend that I would buy a matinee ticket to see a film. Then, as I explained earlier, I upgraded to things like solo restaurant meals and even trips abroad. The more I exposed myself to alone time in public, the braver I became, so this is the approach that I would recommend, rather than diving straight in and putting yourself off.

Technique 2: Take a prop

What I mean by a prop is something like a book or a newspaper or a notepad. This acts as a sort of security blanket that makes you feel more comfortable with the fact that you're by yourself. This is just a way to ease you in so you're not staring into space, worrying about how you might look. I would just make sure that this prop isn't your phone, because it's just such an all-consuming distraction machine. Besides, you did this big brave thing going out with yourself – don't make your date your phone.

Technique 3: Be mindful and engage

When you are without a companion, you're so much more likely to be at one with the activity that you're doing; feel the sensation of your feet hitting the ground when you're out for a walk, sit there and savour that meal, or really enjoy that movie without the sound of your companion crunching popcorn beside you. Know that this is a time for you to engage and be mindful of the experience and reap the benefits of that.

Technique 4: Be unapologetic

I was inspired by the food writer Felicity Cloake for this one. She told me that often when she went to a restaurant by herself, she was shoved in the corner, next to the toilet or in a seat that was less desirable, and she decided it was a sign of respect to her solo experience to always ask for a better table and not feel afraid or ashamed of doing that. That is the kind of energy I want you to be taking into your solo dates.

Solitude skill 4: Communicating alonement

It's important to learn how to communicate your alone time to other people because, remember, alonement isn't something that exists in isolation. Our relationships with other people are hugely important for our wellbeing, and we don't want to alienate them on this journey of learning to spend more time alone. What's really important is learning to effectively and respectfully communicate what you're doing, and let the people who you love, care about and live with know that it's not a rejection of them. Now, it's totally understandable that this might be difficult at first – and take it from me, I'm someone who never used to understand why anyone would practise alone time. Quite often we have different expectations or attitudes towards it in our relationships, and these need to be expressed.

Thankfully, there are ways to get around this communication gap. I was inspired when I had the model Jada Sezer on my podcast. She spoke about how she established really healthy boundaries around this when she first started dating her partner. She told me about how they had a very honest conversation in the first month of their relationship about the non-negotiable time that they wanted to have each week to be with their friends or simply to be alone doing the things they loved to do. That set a really important foundation, as well as helping them to respect and honour each other's desire for alone time. If you can bring that level of communication into your conversations with other people, then it can really help to avoid any awkward moments.

Another great way to communicate on an everyday basis is to talk about your alone time using wording that shows it's not about the other person. Avoid situations where you're slamming a door and saying, 'I need space.' What is better is to say, 'I just fancy some me-time this evening,' or 'I am craving some alonement,' or 'I just need an hour or two to re-energise.' You might also try being specific about the things you want to do: 'I'm going to go for a run this evening,' or 'I'm going to spend some time binge-watching *Gossip Girl*.' It becomes this intrinsic understanding that these are simply the things you do for yourself to re-energise and help you be your best, most giving self.

Solitude skill 5: Balancing solo and social time

We all thrive on a balance of being alone and around other people, and you probably instinctively know this already. But a few years ago, an Israeli study found that each state – solo time and social time – has respective psychological benefits that underpin your wellbeing. So when we're alone, we end up being a bit more reflective, we have a chance to relax from social time and we get round to practising our individual hobbies and interests. Whereas when we're in company, we are on average a bit less likely to slide into feelings of sadness and loneliness, and we are able to be engaged in the present moment a little bit more. Essentially, this shows that you need to honour both states in order to be your most happy, fulfilled self.

And of course, as we know, this balance might vary for everyone – it's not fifty-fifty. Some people are more extroverted and they might like to be around other people most of the time but really benefit from five or ten minutes of solitude every day. Whereas some people are much more introverted and really benefit from time alone a few hours a day to regroup. It's all about being mindful of your energy, through exercises like journaling, and learning what balance works for you.

Establishing and keeping that balance is a lifelong process, but it helps to create daily or weekly rituals around your solo time. For instance, this might just be getting up twenty minutes earlier than your partner so you've got time built into your day where you can be alone first thing in the morning. It really is just about making sure that's planned in.

Be mindful that what works for you won't work for everyone else. Take Sunday evenings, for example. Some people I know love to keep these totally free to do laundry or plan their meals for the week ahead, or simply just regroup before a working week. Whereas personally, if a friend wants to join me for a movie night on a Sunday, I'm all for it. Notice what energises you at certain times of the week, and also make space for the fact that this balance will shift and change depending on your life stage. The important thing to remember is that alone time is something worth valuing.

16. Is it a decision or a habit?

Many of the things we do in a normal day require us to engage our brains, weigh up pros and cons and make an active choice: what we'll have for lunch, for example, or how we'll tackle that work project. But there are only so many decisions we can make in a day before our brains start to weary, which is when the decision's less conscious cousin comes in: the habit. Our habits are our brains way of automating things we've done before, to save energy, and they kick in most strongly when we're overworked and low on decision-making juice.

Both active decisions and autopilot habits impact our lives immeasurably, dictating everything from where we live to what we eat to who we spend our time with, and yet lots of us resign ourselves to the belief that they are largely out of our hands. That we are simply just decisive or indecisive, prone to good habits or perpetually unable to kick the bad ones.

The truth is, the quality of the decisions we make and the habits we perform on a loop can be manipulated and improved with just a few simple techniques, plus a greater understanding of how our brains have evolved to keep us heading through life as efficiently as possible. This chapter will help you learn how to work with your biology and use your finite mental resources in a smarter way, to make better choices for you.

Creatures of habit

Your habits are the behaviours or routines you barely think about, ingrained impulses that cause you to do things in response to triggers or cues. For example, you wake up and you go to the bathroom to brush your teeth on autopilot, all while you're thinking about what pastry you'll pick up on the way to the office.

Then there are the bad habits you want to kick, whether it's indulging in some late-night doomscrolling or biting your nails. Yet despite being able to identify the flaws in our ways, knowing how bad they are for us and disliking the consequences of our actions, we continue. Why?

The answer, it seems, lies in our brain chemistry. Our bad habits are the product of the brain's subconscious: psychological shortcuts that allow us to save energy and solve problems based on what we already know. 'The brain is always looking for ways to conserve its resources, and therefore if you repeat an action enough times, your brain creates a neural pathway,' explains Dr Sophie Mort, a clinical psychologist and also known as 'Dr Soph'. 'These connections can be activated simply by: one, seeing the person, place or thing, that would usually cause you to start that action; or two, feeling something inside you that would cause you to do the same. If you have been driving for a long time, you will notice that you can drive without much thought, chatting away to your friend sitting next to you or singing along to the radio at the same time. This is because the car, and the environment of the road, is cuing each appropriate driving behaviour. Unless something happens that is totally out of the blue, you can keep driving in this habitual way to your destination.'

She offers another example you may recognise. 'If you are a

seasoned phone scroller, you may notice that every time you feel bored, lonely or stressed, or simply see your phone, you reach for it. This is an example of how a mix of internal and environmental cues can trigger habitual actions.'

This ability for our brains to set our bodies to autopilot is quite incredible, and incredibly useful. 'Habits help you do almost everything you do each day. They help you get out of bed, get dressed, brush your teeth, know to smile at your loved ones when you see them or if you want to show that you like what they said. They are solutions to life's problems,' says Dr Soph. However, she adds, they can also be a problem at times. 'They may also cause issues for you if they take you away from the person you wish to be (e.g. if you procrastinate every time you have something challenging to do, or constantly press snooze in the morning to the point where you are late every day), or if they are dangerous (e.g. if you find yourself texting and driving as the mix of your phone-checking habit cuts into your driving, leading you to stop focusing on the road).

'The thing is, entrenched habits will continue whether you want them to or not, if you don't do anything targeted to change them. For example, you will smoke, drink and check your phone even if you don't fancy it in that moment, if you have enough cues in your environment to make you keep doing it, and if you don't have a plan to put a stop to the habit.

'Habits are formed most quickly when the action gives us a strong internal reward (e.g. a burst of dopamine, as in the case of some drugs) or resolution (e.g. the immediate removal of feelings of anxiety or loneliness, as can also happen with drugs or alcohol). And sometimes habits can be formed faster than we would imagine.'

It makes total sense that our brains are always reaching for ways to make us feel good, but it's worth noting that on the most extreme end of the spectrum, this is the basis of addiction, and if you worry that your habits are more like compulsions you can't control, it's important you speak to a trained professional (visit mind.org for advice).

What we get wrong about habits

'The most common misconceptions when it comes to habits include the idea that it takes twenty-one days to form one,' says Dr Soph. 'It would be lovely if this was the case, but the research says it takes sixty-six days on average, and this can vary widely between eighteen and 254 days. There are a number of factors that affect how long it will take to create a new habit, including how rewarding or pleasurable you find the activity, and the number of times you repeat the activity.

'Another misconception is that all repeated activities will become habits. This is unfortunately not the case. Routines are the actions we repeat over and over. We have to think about them. Habits in the scientific sense are automatic and triggered by cues, either in our environment or feelings inside us. All habits start out as routines.

'For example, when you learned to drive, brush your teeth or use your phone, you were performing one action after the other. Reminding yourself of what you had to do at each step, until these things became habitual. But not all routines will become habits – some tasks might always remain routine. Particularly if we find them effortful, unpleasant or unrewarding. This is important to know, as I often hear people say, "I can't create habits, as I still have to remind myself to brush my teeth", or "There must be something wrong with me, as I still have to have an accountability buddy to make sure I go to the gym, even after going for over two years". People then assume that there is no hope, or they beat themselves up. But this is not necessarily the case; you are probably just performing routines.'

How to break an unwanted habit

Hit the brakes

If our bad habits are deeply buried in our subconscious, what exactly can we do about them? The first step is surprisingly simple. To break our bad habits, we need to constantly remind ourselves of these subconscious processes, and 'get out of the backseat' when it comes to our daily decision-making. By being more mindful of the little actions we take, whether that's what snack we're going to eat or when we're going to spend time on our phones, we can overthrow those automatic responses which have weaved their way into our brains.

Even if they feel trivial, bring your attention to the little things you do that feel automatic. Ask yourself: *Why am I compelled to say yes to that offer of another round of drinks? Why am I picking up my phone right now? Why am I clicking 'next episode' even though it's late and I'm yawning?* Often, the answer can be found on a physiological level – your body is craving a hit of dopamine, the 'reward' chemical that feels good in the moment but always leaves us wanting more. That simple act of bringing your attention to what you're doing on autopilot breaks your habitual thought patterns and gives you a moment to assess whether it's something you really want to do, or it's just something you *usually* do.

Identify your why

'Ask yourself, why do you want to quit this habit?' says Dr Soph. 'How will quitting it help you in the long run? Identity is a great motivator. Also, getting clear on your why is important as we almost always sabotage ourselves when we try to do something that we don't really want to do.'

Observe yourself

'Spend the next forty-eight hours observing the habit you want to quit,' advises Dr Soph. 'Look for all the cues that cause you to engage in that behaviour – for example, if you want to break your constant phone-checking habit, look for what triggers you to reach for it. List each reason, whether it's external (seeing it, hearing it beep) or internal (feeling bored, in need of a break or stressed). Then pay attention to how you feel during and after the habitual action – what resolution/reward are you getting? If it's picking up your phone, it may be that it makes you feel connected, stimulated or amused. List these outcomes too.'

Cut your cues

'Next,' says Dr Soph, 'decide which of the cues you can remove from your environment. Can you hide your phone so you can't see it? Can you turn off notifications so it doesn't cut into your productive periods? Then decide what alternative actions you could engage in to meet your internal cues and cravings. If you notice you are bored, in need of a break or stressed, will you get up from your desk or wherever you are and go for a walk? Will you do some stretches or take a moment of meditation or physiological sighing (see page 195)? Remove the cues you can, then write a note and set it in front of you. It might say something like, "When I notice I feel [insert internal cue here], I will get up and do [the other activity to achieve the resolution you require]."'

Stop and reset

'Whenever you catch yourself in your old habit, immediately move to your replacement,' Dr Soph says. 'Put the phone down and commence the alternative activity you planned. Over time, the cue will become paired with your new activity and you will create your new and desired habit even if you fall off the wagon, so to speak.'

How to kick the most common bad habit there is – always being late

Being a late person is something you might consider an unfortunate, but inevitable, part of your personality. Always rushing for a train even after promising yourself to leave five minutes earlier, missing appointments, or being the member of your family or friendship group who others simply expect to turn up at least fifteen minutes after everyone else. If any of this is sounding painfully relatable, you probably don't need anyone to tell you just how much being late can negatively impact your life.

Being late may seem like a big part of the way you live your life, but there are some ways in which you can change that. Typical advice for those who are late often comes from people who already have brilliant timekeeping skills and have no idea what it's like to constantly turn up late for things, even after taking several steps to avoid it. That's why Grace G. Pacie, who has been a late person for her entire life, wrote the book, *Late: A Timebender's Guide to Why We Are Late and How We Can Change*, providing practical advice for late people that actually works.

Pacie has identified seven common reasons why people are late. If you can figure out which of these are relevant to you, you might just be able to start getting over your lateness for good, with the help of Pacie's expert advice.

Seven reasons why you're late

1. You hesitate to finish things

'One reason why you might end up being late is that you don't close things down until the last minute, and once you're stuck into something, you don't want to move on,' Pacie says. She explains that this often leads to you frantically running around at the last minute.

2. You don't like being early

'You probably always tell yourself that you'll be early next time, but you always end up delaying leaving on time, squeezing in one more thing before you leave,' Pacie says. She adds that you might also find the experience of being early and/or being the first person at an event uncomfortable and boring, so part of you is avoiding it.

3. You're not good at measuring time

'Late people often miscalculate timings,' Pacie says, explaining that, often, you probably think you have enough time to get ready and do everything else you need to do before leaving the house, but it turns out that you don't.

4. You need real deadlines with consequences

'Deadlines are a great tool for late people but they have to be real,' Pacie says. 'If you tell yourself you need to be somewhere by a certain time but no one is holding you to account and there's no consequences, it doesn't mean anything to you.'

5. You don't leave any transition time

'In your head, maybe you think you can just drop what you're doing and be where you need to be in no time, not taking into account the two minutes it takes you to walk from one room to another and wash a dish, for example,' Pacie says. She explains that these short transition times add up and might eventually cause you to be late.

6. You're a complete optimist

'You probably assume that all the lights are going to be green and all the roads will be empty on your journey,' Pacie says, adding that a common reason that people end up being late is that they 'don't leave time for things to go wrong'.

7. You do things back to front

'Until your deadline is imminent, you're probably prioritising doing less important things before doing the things that really need to be done,' Pacie says, explaining that most late people won't do the things that are absolutely essential until just before they need to leave.

So how do you stop being late?

Know that if you can be on time when it matters, you can always be on time

'Late people often say that they can be on time when it matters, like when they're catching a flight,' Pacie says. 'If this is the case and you do have the capability to be on time, there's no reason why you shouldn't be able to do it all the time. Maybe you have a secret scale of acceptable lateness. You'll allow yourself to be late for most things even if you always meet strict deadlines.'

Pacie explains that you need to refigure how you perceive the things in your life that you're often late for and ask yourself, 'Why am I not treating these things as important?' Once you recognise the value of something, you can motivate yourself to be on time for it.

Think about how your actions affect the people around you

'Being late might not be causing huge problems for you, but it's definitely causing problems for the people in your life,' Pacie says. She explains that the people who you're late for are the people who have to bear the brunt of your actions, and this can cause real tension in relationships.

'If you can put the focus on other people and how you're making them feel, rather than yourself, you feel more encouraged to change your ways,' Pacie adds.

Recognise the importance of deadlines and create them for yourself

Late people tend to only be able to stick to deadlines if they have real consequences, so find ways to do this. 'Involve other people in your deadline,' Pacie suggests, explaining that you could offer someone a lift or arrange to meet another person before arriving at an event. 'When other people are involved, it becomes real,' she says. 'You could also commit to some sort of penalty or forfeit if you don't meet your deadline.' One example of a penalty she has found to be effective is committing to donating to a charity you don't believe in if you don't meet your deadline. 'You should also set an earlier deadline before your event or commitment, like going to get a coffee on your way out or dropping something off at the post office,' Pacie says. 'You might miss your first deadline, but you're less likely to miss the thing that really matters.'

Prepare for being early
You probably know that you should always plan to get somewhere ten to fifteen minutes before you need to, in case of complications on the way. But maybe your fear of being early is holding you back from doing this. 'In that case, make sure you've planned something that you can do in case you are early, whether it's reading a book or answering emails,' Pacie says. You should make this task something you actually want or need to do, so you know the time spent being early won't be wasted.

How to create good habits that stick

Starting new habits can feel so hard because we're going against our brain's natural tendency to keep us on autopilot, but it's not impossible. The good news is, we can apply what we know about 'bad' habits to help us create good ones. As Dr Soph says, habits start with routines, plus a few extra considerations that will help create those new neural pathways. 'Firstly, always try to set up your environment so that your routine is easy to perform,' she says. This could look like setting up everything you need to wake up, get dressed and head straight out for a walk in the morning.

'Then support the routine in other ways,' Dr Soph continues. 'For example, by enlisting the support of friends to do the routines with you, increasing enjoyment, motivation and accountability, or including keystone habits that have wider-reaching effects than the actions themselves. That might be working on daily planning and a "do the hardest things on your list first" habit, so that you know what you have to do each day and when. It's also strengthening the muscle of turning towards the tasks you would instinctually like to avoid, i.e. the effortful, unpleasant ones, which are the ones most likely to take the longest to make into habit.'

Finally, says Dr Soph, cut yourself some slack. 'Don't berate yourself for the effortful nature of the task,' she says. 'Remember that just because something hasn't become automatic after a long time of practising it, it doesn't mean it never will.'

Here's her checklist for creating new healthy habits.

- Decide who you will be in the future if you maintain this habit (this gives you your 'why', which is very motivating).
- Decide which part of the day to work your new habit into (quick tip: your brain chemistry is set up to help you face challenges in the first eight hours of the day – that is, if you aren't a night-shift worker or a new parent – and therefore all new activities that

you may want to resist should go in these first eight hours until they are habitual).

- Decide what cues will remind you to do this habit and put them in your environment. For example, put your mindfulness app on your phone, or put your exercise gear next to your bed so it is the first thing you see when you wake up.

- Break down the activity into its smallest parts (e.g. 'I will meditate for ten minutes every day; I will exercise for ten minutes, three days a week'). Then decide what activity you will stack this new activity on top of. Instead of saying, 'I will do X at 9am,' instead say, 'After I brush my teeth, I will do X,' or 'When I wake up, I will put on my exercise clothes, then I will have my usual cup of coffee. The moment I have finished that, I will immediately go for a run.'

- Enlist the support of friends and see if you can get them onboard with the activity too, so you can all support each other in creating a habit.

- Decide on how you will reward your new activity, but make your rewards intermittent. For example, you might flip a coin after you complete your meditation or run, to see whether you get whatever it is you decided would be a fun boost after your new activity. This is based on a psychological finding that we tend to keep coming back to habits that *may* offer us a reward but don't guarantee it. The unpredictability is part of the draw to try again. Then practise. Practise, practise and practise some more.

Dr Soph's number-one tip for creating a habit

'If you were to ask me what is the one thing that makes a habit the
most likely to stick, it is simply repeating the beginning of the
action as often as you can. Focusing on the instigation element of
the habit, just getting started, or leaving the house, or whatever
the initial step is, is more important than what you do when you
complete the habit itself. Repeat turning the meditation on and
sitting down to listen to it, or running out of your door as often as
you can. At some point, this will become habitual.'

Decisions, decisions . . .

Allow us to set the scene. Sitting in front of the TV, you scroll through
the endless options of what to watch while your dinner turns cold on
your lap. The longer you spend trying to decide, the higher the stakes
become. The working day has left your head buzzing, and you could
do with some soothing escapism. But, as the minutes tick by, you just
cannot choose. Nothing seems worth the commitment. You're
overwhelmed. Eventually, you switch off the TV and dig into your
congealed meal in a huff. Been there?

It's a classic example of how options – limitless, instantly accessible
options like the ones all around us in our tech-fuelled world – aren't
always a good thing. At first, it's a counterintuitive thought. Surely the
more choice we have, the more likely we are to find something that
will make us happy, right? But science, plus that feeling of choice
overwhelm that's increasingly familiar, say otherwise.

In fact, back in 2000, two scientists from Stanford University conducted a study that proved what had long been suspected. They set up display tables at a food market; one had twenty-four varieties of jam for sale, the other had just six. The study found that while the larger display generated more initial interest, the customers were far less likely to buy a jar from that table than those who visited the smaller display. The study holds huge sway in the marketing world, but it tells us something interesting about how our minds work, too: although an abundance of choice seems appealing at first, it's not necessarily conducive to making a decision. When you consider the fact that Netflix alone offers more than 7,000 films and programmes – too many to get through in a lifetime – it begs the question: does modern life offer up more choice than our brains can actually handle?

Those of us who have a smartphone (eighty-eight per cent of UK adults as of 2021) quite literally have the world at our fingertips, with practically every song, book, recipe, film or idea in history available for our consideration. Some of the websites we buy clothes from add hundreds of new items every day. The different world cuisines we can order steaming hot to our doors seem to multiply constantly. This level of convenience has been life-changing and world-expanding, but there is a hidden cost: it requires a huge amount of decision-making.

The average person now spends 148 minutes a day weighing up decisions, according to a study by Barclays and University College London, and more than forty per cent of us report feeling stressed or anxious when we do. On your next commute, try doing a mental roll call of the choices you've been faced with before you even sit down at your desk. Get up or hit snooze? Trainers or boots? Latte or flat white? Which font to use on this Instagram story? Which emoji feels right for that message? Each one might not feel that challenging in the moment, but together they can rack up and leave us mentally drained. You might recognise a tipping point: your partner asks you what you want for dinner and suddenly you feel your head might explode.

The curse of decision fatigue

Mental energy is a finite resource, and making a decision is one of the most complex mental processes there is. Information relating to memories, emotions and external context are gathered from every area of the brain and sent to the prefrontal cortex to be processed, all in a matter of milliseconds, every time we're faced with a dilemma. It follows that the more decisions we have to make in a day, the more tired our brains get – and the worse we get at making them.

This phenomenon has been dubbed 'decision fatigue' by the neuroscientific world, and it has been demonstrated in some interesting studies. One conducted by researchers at Ben-Gurion University looked at parole judges: at the beginning of their court sessions, they were much more likely to make bolder decisions about the offenders they were considering, i.e. granting them release, whereas near the end, they tended to play it safe and deny parole, the mental fatigue warping their ability to judge well and therefore nudging them to take the easy way out.

The fact is, when we've been tasked with making lots of decisions throughout the day, each subsequent choice becomes harder to properly parse. It's why 'impulse purchases' and sweet snacks are often displayed next to the till in your local supermarket, after you've already made countless choices about what to buy for the week ahead and are now extra susceptible to grabbing something without thinking through whether you really want it. In the context of the weekly shop it might not seem like a big deal, but when it comes to making good choices for everything from your wellbeing to that major project at work, it's crucial to know when and where you can mitigate the impact of decision fatigue in your daily life.

Five ways to limit decision fatigue

1. Prioritise

Ever sat staring at your growing pile of unread emails or jumbled to-do list and just felt paralysed, like you don't even know where to start? It's more than procrastination – when you sit in front of a large number of tasks that require your attention with no sense of which to prioritise, it's a recipe for choice overwhelm. Try setting aside five minutes in the morning to review what you need to get done that day and write a list in order of most urgent to least, as well as a realistic estimate of how long each task will take you. You'll be amazed at how not having to make the decision about what to focus on next after each task will help you glide through them seamlessly.

2. Plan ahead

There's a reason some of the greatest minds and most successful figureheads of our time have had strict morning routines and daily uniforms. In an interview with *Vanity Fair* during his tenure as US President, Barack Obama summed it up: 'You'll see I wear only grey or blue suits. I'm trying to pare down decisions,' he said. 'I don't want to make decisions about what I'm eating or wearing, because I have too many other decisions to make.'

Making some of the choices we're faced with every day completely automatic means we're conserving mental energy from the moment we wake up. Simplifying your wardrobe, preparing a breakfast like overnight oats or a smoothie the day before, and laying out your gear for a morning run before you sleep are all brilliant ways to limit decisions. If you know you've got a full-on week coming up and you need to be on your A-game, go one further and plot out exactly what you need to do each day in a diary or planner that is easy to refer back to. It sounds simple, but it can be transformative to know your schedule is already pre-ordained and all you need to do is follow it.

3. Delegate

Help is at hand far more than most of us realise, and it's in your interest to take it where you can when it comes to decision-making. At work, try to maintain limits around what you absolutely need to sign off on and what you can delegate to a colleague or team member – often, people respond well to that level of trust and responsibility, so don't feel guilty about it. Same goes for your family and friends; when there is something you feel you don't have the time or mental capacity for, your first port of call should be to ask if a loved one does have the capacity, or to see if they can at least help you reach a decision. If you arranged the meet-up, you're well within your rights to ask someone else to pick the restaurant.

4. Lean on the experts

Often, the decisions that are the most taxing are the ones we don't feel fully equipped to make. This is where we should lean in to the expertise of others for advice, whether that's crowdsourcing suggestions from another team at work or buying into one of the many curated offerings in the world of food, fashion and entertainment now. For example, if you find shopping for clothes an overwhelming experience, there are shopping services such as Stitch Fix, which selects ten items for you to try on at home based on your personal style. If what to watch leaves you stumped, you can browse Flixi, an app that uses AI to track what you watch and offer recommendations, or Decider.com, where culture experts offer picks based on your mood.

5. Commit to the choice

The fact that we have so much more choice than we used to means it's easy to double back on yourself. You might watch ten minutes of a film at home only to change your mind and start something else. This chopping and changing only adds to the number of decisions we're making in a day, and takes us further away from making a satisfying one, which is ironic but vital to remember the next time you want to change your mind. Chances are, sticking with what you've chosen will give you a better outcome.

When you have to make a choice, here's how to make a good one

Now that your brain is freed up to focus on the more important decisions, it's worth having a mental toolkit to call upon if you often find that committing to a choice is difficult for you, or you worry that you don't always consider them from all the necessary angles. It's worth noting that no one is an innately 'good' or 'bad' decision-maker – a myth we often tell ourselves and others – and everyone has the same ability to be decisive. It's really more about how we 'spend' the brainpower we have. For example, think of someone you see as wise and trustworthy in the face of an on-the-spot choice; chances are they have healthy habits and routines that help them conserve mental energy. Here are some techniques you can put in place to become a better decider, too.

Home in on the ideal result

Focusing on exactly what you'd like your decision to result in can help you make a better, more informed choice. Where to meet a friend for a drink is a classic; the options may be limitless. But once you start asking yourself pointed questions, it'll become much clearer to decide. Do you want somewhere quiet or a buzzier vibe? Would you like it to be a new experience or the cosy comfort of somewhere you've been before? Do you want to be in bed early, meaning it shouldn't be too far from home? Think about what kind of night you want to have, and work backwards from there.

Get a second, third and fourth opinion

For the bigger decisions in life, we can ruminate on them for so long that we forget to outsource at all, but other people's opinions can be very valuable in offering perspective. Thinking about getting a pet? Your mind might be full of all the positives – the snuggles! The walks! – but asking a few people who know you well will help you see the reasons it may not work out, too. It's helpful to ask people individually rather than in a group so they can speak their mind without any outside influence.

Make a pros and cons list

It's a classic decision-making tool for a reason; the very act of putting pen to paper can clarify your thoughts. Write down everything that comes to mind and then review it with a critical eye – which side of the chart really seems to outweigh the other?

Make tough decisions in the morning

The very nature of decision fatigue means our brains are typically at their most refreshed and ready to take on challenges an hour or so after we wake up. If you have a big decision to make, such as who to hire for your team or whether to put in an offer on that new flat, try to set aside time to think it through early in the day. You're much more likely to make bold, considered decisions rather than lazy ones.

A final word

So you've come to the end of *How to Be Curious*, but I hope it's just the beginning. When it comes to the big things – our wellbeing, our work and our relationships – there is always more to dig in to, more to discover about what makes us tick and how we can use that self-knowledge to live happier, fuller lives.

This book offers an introduction to these all-important topics, but I hope it has challenged you to ask some new questions about yourself: the most interesting and worthy topic of all. I hope, too, that it has satisfied some of your natural curiosity. You may have begun to think more deeply about your professional ambitions, and what a successful working life really looks like for you without the expectations or influences of anyone else. Perhaps you've taken a closer look at your relationships and the dynamics within them, or felt inspired to strike up some new ones. Maybe you've discovered some wellbeing practices, from mindfulness to biohacking, that feel like a good fit. Or perhaps you've come away with greater understanding of your sleep chronotype, or your attachment style, or just why that habit you keep trying to instate isn't quite sticking.

Whatever you take from this book, I hope that it's just the start of your curious journey, and that you keep its pages and all the generously given expert knowledge within them by your side as a companion whenever you feel yourself stuck in a rut. Keep asking the questions that matter, and stay open to learning something new.

Meena Alexander, Features Director of *Stylist*

References

RELATIONSHIPS

1. Should friendships be hard work?
Northwestern Medicine. 'Aging well: the value of friendship', 2019, nm.org.

Snap. 'Celebrating friendship with the friendship report', 2019, newsroom.snap.com.

Kamarck, T. W., Manuck, S. B. and Jennings, J. R. 'Social support reduces cardiovascular reactivity to psychological challenge: a laboratory model', *Psychosomatic Medicine*, vol. 52, no. 1, 1990, pp. 42–58.

Giles, Lynne, *et al.* 'Effect of social networks on 10-year survival in very old Australians: the Australian longitudinal study of aging', *Journal of Epidemiology and Health*, vol. 59, no. 7, 2005, pp. 574–9.

Office for National Statistics. 'National life tables – life expectancy in the UK: 2018 to 2020', ons.gov.uk, 2021.

Kagan, Paula. 'Feeling listened to: a lived experience of human becoming', *Nursing Science Quarterly*, vol. 21, no. 1, 2008, pp. 59–67.

3. Why boundaries aren't about other people
VanVonderen, Jeff. *Tired of Trying to Measure Up: Getting Free From the Demands, Expectations and Intimidation of Well-Meaning People*, Bethany House Publishers, 2008.

WORK

5. The shifting shape of ambition

Office for National Statistics. 'Average actual weekly hours of work for full-time workers (seasonally adjusted)', 2023, ons.gov.uk.

Sisterhood and After Research Team, British Library. 'Education and the Women's Liberation Movement', 2013, bl.uk.

Watson, Erika and Pearson, Ruth. 'Here to Stay: Women's self-employment in a (post) austerity era', 2015, Women's Budget Group, wbg.org.uk.

Andrew, Alison, et al. 'Working paper: The gendered division of paid and domestic work under lockdown', 2021, ifs.org.uk.

Health and Safety Executive, 'Press release: HSE published annual work-related ill-health and injury statistics for 2021/22', 2022, hse.gov.uk.

6. Boredom as a superpower

Wilson, Timothy, et al. 'Just think: the challenges of the disengaged mind', Science, vol. 345, no. 6192, 2014, pp.75–7.

Mann, Mary. Yawn: Adventures in Boredom, Farrar, Strauss & Giroux, 2017.

CV-Library. 'How to stop boredom at work', 2017, cv-library.co.uk.

7. Deep-work or time blocking? Find your productivity personality

Wu Tsai Neurosciences Institute, Stanford University. 'Why multitasking does more harm than good', 2021, neuroscience.stanford.edu.

8. Why your emotions should run your career

Lewis, Liz. 'Workplace wellbeing insights from the 2021 world happiness report', 2021, uk.indeed.com.

Aviva. 'Number of UK workers planning career changes rises', 2021, aviva.com.

WELLBEING

9. Why mindfulness is *not* meditation
Bilton, Nick. 'Part of the daily American diet: 34 gigabytes of data', *New York Times*, 9 December 2009.

Mehrabian, Albert. *Nonverbal Communication*, Taylor & Francis 1972.

10. Good stress, bad stress
Pratt, Louron. 'New studies find that 90% of the UK workers are stressed most of the time', 2019, hrdconnect.com.

Mental Health Foundation. 'Stressed nation: 74% of UK "overwhelmed or unable to cope" at some point in the past year', 2018, mentalhealth.org.uk.

The Decision Lab. 'The ABC model', thedecisionlab.com.

11. This chapter will change the way you rest
Mintel. 'Mintel announces global consumer trends for 2021', 2022, mintel.com.

Kirk, Isabelle. 'One in eight Britons feel tired all the time', 2022, yougov.co.uk.

Dalton-Smith, Saundra. *Sacred Rest: Recover Your Life, Renew Your Energy, Restore Your Sanity*, Time Warner, 2019.

Francis, Gemma. 'Average Briton spends seven and a half years feeling tired, study suggests', *Independent*, 14 March 2018.

Breus, Michael. 'Chronotypes', 2023, sleepdoctor.com.

King's College London. 'How the UK is sleeping under lockdown', 2020, kcl.ac.uk.

MacNaught, Michael. 'The state of annual leave – statistics for 2022 & 2023', 2023, timetastic.com.

Institute of Leadership. 'New survey by the ILM finds 61% of workers feel obligated to work whilst on holiday', 2021, leadership.global.

YOU

13. Breaking the comparison curse

Royal Society for Public Health. '#StatusOfMind: Social media and young people's mental health and wellbeing', 2017, rsph.org.uk.

de Waal, Frans B. M. 'Joint ventures require joint payoffs: fairness among primates', *Social Research*, vol. 73, no. 2, 2006, pp. 349–64.

Kahneman, Daniel, and Deaton, Angus. 'High income improves evaluation of life but not wellbeing', *Proceedings of the National Academy of Sciences of the United States of America*, vol. 107, no. 38, 2010, pp. 16489–93.

Geall, Lauren. 'How social media is changing the way we see our relationships', *Stylist*, 2019.

Emmons Faculty. 'Gratitude and wellbeing: summary of findings', emmons. faculty.ucdavis.edu.

American Psychological Association. 'Reducing social media use significantly improves body image in teens, young adults', 2023, apa.org.

14. How to be more confident in the ways that matter

Saha Roy, Tiasha, Mazumder, Satyaki, and Das, Koel. 'Wisdom of crowds benefits perceptual decision-making across difficulty levels', *Scientific Reports*, vol. 11, no. 538, 2021.

McCrea, Simon. 'Intuition, insight and the right hemisphere: Emergence of higher sociocognitive functions', *Psychology Research and Behaviour Management*, vol. 3, 2010, pp. 1–39.

15. How to thrive alone

Thomas, Virginia. 'The psychological affordances of solitude in emerging adulthood', *Emerging Adulthood*, vol. 11, no. 3, 2023, pp. 611–25.

Specter, Francesca (host). 'Jada Sezer', *Alonement,* season 1, episode 3, 20 March 2020.

16. Is it a decision or a habit?

Iyengar, S. and Lepper, M. R. 'When choice is demotivating: can one desire too much of a good thing?', *Journal of Personality and Social Psychology*, vol. 79, no. 6, 2000, pp. 995–1006.

Hiley, Catherine. 'UK mobile phone statistics, 2023', 2023, uswitch.com.

Barclays. 'Press release: The decision dilemma: the everyday decisions that eat up our time', 2020, home.barclays.

Danziger, S., Levav, J. and Avnaim-Pesso, L. 'Extraneous factors in judicial decisions', *PNAS*, vol. 108, no. 17, 2011, pp. 6889–92.

Vanity Fair. 'Barack Obama to Michael Lewis on a presidential loss of freedom: "You don't get used to it – at least, I don't"', 2012, vanityfair.com.

Acknowledgements

A huge and heartfelt thank you to every professor, doctor and expert in their field who generously lent their time and insight to this book and allowed me to share their wise words and exciting ideas in its pages. Thank you to the editors and writers behind The Curiosity Academy, Alex Sims and Alice Porter, who helped bring to life the concept that acted as a springboard for *How To Be Curious*, and who worked on some of the interviews repurposed for its publication. I'm very grateful to Lindsey Evans and Kate Miles at Headline Home – without you this collection wouldn't exist – and for the sharp eye and patience of Tara O'Sullivan. Last but not least, a shout out to *Stylist*'s editorial director Lisa Smosarski, who in 2009 launched exactly the kind of smart, sensitive and celebratory media brand I'd been waiting my whole life for. Thank you for entrusting me with a small piece of your very special legacy.

Index